OCCUPY!

VERSO

This edition first published by Verso 2011
Featuring content from *Occupy! Gazette*
The collection © Verso 2011
Individual contributions © The contributors 2011
All rights reserved

1 3 5 7 9 10 8 6 4 2

Verso
UK 6 Meard Street, London W1F 0EG
US: 20 Jay Street, Suite 1010, Brooklyn, NY 11201
www.versobooks.com

Verso is the imprint of New Left Books

N+1
68 Jay Street, Suite 405, Brooklyn, NY 11201
www.nplusonemag.com

ISBN-13: 978-1-84467-940-9

ebook ISBN-13: 978-1-84467-941-6

British Library Cataloguing in Publication Data
A catalogue record for this book is available from the British Library

Library of Congress Cataloging-in-Publication Data
A catalog record for this book is available from the Library of Congress

Layout and typography by Rumors
Printed in the US by Maple Vail

OCCUPY!

SCENES
FROM
OCCUPIED
AMERICA

Edited by Astra Taylor, Keith Gessen, and editors from *n+1*,
Dissent, Triple Canopy and *The New Inquiry*

Dan Archer, "Occupied Oakland"

Josh MacPhee

PREFACE

The genesis of this book is that we were lucky enough to be in New York, and in America, at the start of the occupations of public ground that began in September 2011. We started as participant-observers. None of us thought this protest would be anything bigger than others we had joined. As time went on, we became observers more explicitly. Something was unfolding, which was becoming one of the most significant and hopeful events of our lifetimes.

We started with what we know how to do. We wrote, we got our friends to write, we edited, and we compiled. Soon we had a broadsheet newspaper, a sort of living document that we distributed for free around the city and online. Our first two OWS-inspired *Gazettes* formed the basis of this book.

The diaries come through our eyes, with inevitable traces of the ways we see and think and dream. Like all documentation of the movement, there is nothing official about this record. The essays represent other views we solicited, ideas we sought, and speeches we heard. As the weeks went on, we realized we wanted to leave something for the future to hold, a prism to put to the lamp of the event.

As this book went to press, during what seems to be part of a crackdown on occupations across the country, Zuccotti Park/Liberty Plaza was raided. Following the example of police in other cities, the NYPD entered the camp under cover of night and evicted all the residents, confiscating tents, sleeping bags, and books, and pepper-spraying and arresting protesters. In response to these attacks, occupiers posted a message online. "You can't evict an idea whose time has come," it began. Rebecca Solnit put it more poetically: "You can pull up the flowers, but you can't stop the spring."

The movement and this book are not over. We will continue writing updates and analyses on the *Occupy! Gazette* website.

Astra, Eli, Nikil, Sarah R, Sarah L, Mark, Keith, Carla

Illustration by Molly Crabapple

SCENES FROM AN OCCUPA-TION

ELI SCHMITT, ASTRA TAYLOR
& MARK GREIF

Saturday, September 17

Eli:

When I got off the train in the Financial District last Saturday, the first thing I did was accidentally walk into a policeman. He and fifteen or so other policemen were standing in front of a barricade that had been set up to prevent anyone from entering Wall Street. As I backed away, flustered, I heard one member of a passing elderly couple say to the other, pointing between two buildings, "Is that the Freedom Tower going up over there?"

I had come to the Financial District for a gathering of leftist dissidents, an event that had been described to me as an "occupation of Wall Street." There were a few websites explaining that "For #occupywallstreet, dispersion is part of the plan" and informing protesters that they "do not need a permit to occupy or peaceably assemble on public sidewalks." Emails and blog posts alluded to the Supreme Court decision in *Citizens United*, popular uprisings in the Middle East, and the intense clout of financial institutions. The tone of the pieces varied, but all shared a sense of indignation. The event seemed to be predicated on the idea that the act of assembling was threatened, that the gathering was a justification of itself.

I had trouble finding this gathering, however, since Wall Street itself had been shut down. Chase Manhattan Plaza—the designated meeting place—was surrounded by police barriers. At the barricades, I didn't see any protesters, only tourists having their pictures taken with cops and tourists having their pictures taken by cops. It was only 3:30 PM but it felt like dusk. As I walked, I came to suspect that there were no dissidents at all, that any organized group action had been squelched by the hundreds of police guarding the narrow passageways between the skyscrapers.

Finally, a friend responded to my text message and told me where to find the General Assembly. The group had congregated in Zuccotti Park, at Liberty Plaza, a paved rectangle between Broadway and Trinity Place, and looked to be at least a few hundred strong. Instead of a single, unified

ELI SCHMITT, ASTRA TAYLOR & MARK GREIF

congregation, there were smaller circles of ten to fifty people, some with megaphones. Some circles had moderators and agendas, others appeared to be more spontaneous. Speakers took turns sharing their thoughts and suggestions: how we should be respectful to the police ("fuck the police, love the police officer"), how cronyism was destroying our democracy. People—some compelling, others less so—urged one another to storm Wall Street, shared information about where to find food and blankets, and decried the Obama administration. Around the edges of the park, rows of police officers and large groups of protesters milled about.

Astra:

The first day I arrived and surveyed the scene, I was totally dispirited: same old, same old, and not very substantial. Since the authorities had locked down the area in anticipation of the day's events, demonstrators were dispersed and outnumbered by police. But then I followed an impromptu procession into the park where they are now encamped. I hooked up with a group of friends and we had an "assembly" with a bunch of strangers and talked economics for two or three hours. It was kind of nice to be at a protest and, instead of marching and shouting, to be talking about ideas. It felt like the script had changed. As 7 PM approached, my friends and I left thinking the cops would clear everyone out in no time. When they made it through the night I began to give them more credit.

Mark:

It was a nice day. I came to meet a couple of friends, and we ran into people we knew distantly, met up with Astra and her friends, and then ran into people from *Dissent* and from *The New Inquiry*. We joined up, sat down, and did what the organizers asked, which was to discuss which proposals or demands were most important to us, for this collective gathering. These would be put to the General Assembly for public discussion, so this large group of strangers could determine its purpose. Our circle attracted more visitors and strangers.

SCENES FROM AN OCCUPATION

After a series of votes and debates, we concluded that the desire that brought most people in our group together was this: to restore government to citizen control, to regulate finance for the common good, and to get banks out of the business of buying legislators and influencing law. We talked about debt and mortgage relief and the destruction of Glass-Steagall and McCain-Feingold, and what it would take to save their purpose. We'd need the country's agreement that freedom of speech belongs only to living citizens, not corporations—to overturn the *Citizens United* ruling—probably by a movement for a constitutional amendment. That was our proposal! We shared email addresses and resolved to learn how to start. It wasn't until later that I realized it was Constitution Day, the 224th anniversary of its signing before the document went to the states for ratification.

Eli:

Someone suggested that we "assemble," so we all sat down in a circle. It seemed almost like a joke at first. We had to speak loudly to hear each other over the sounds of voices from neighboring assemblies and the occasional police siren. From time to time, a woman seated on a nearby bench rattled a tambourine.

Someone asked what the action was, what we were going to do, and someone else responded that this was the action, that we were there to talk and organize. Someone suggested that we come up with our demands as a group; then, after some deliberation, we decided we should have just one demand. Our job, as a single congregation, was to decide what was most important to us. I agreed to take notes, and as we talked I wrote down the following list of potential demands:

> *To repeal the* Citizens United *Supreme Court decision (through a constitutional amendment)*
> *To remove the bull sculpture from Wall Street (as suggested to us by a man who walked by dressed as a banker but wearing a noose instead of a tie)*

*Some form of debt cancellation (either for everyone or just
    for students)*
*Pay-as-you-go military intervention (so that wars could not
    be waged without Congress agreeing to finance each step
    immediately)*
*Taxes on small financial transactions (one version of this is
    known as a Tobin tax)*
Full employment
*A social wage or guaranteed income (also described as a neg-
    ative income tax)*
Universal care centers (for children and the elderly)
*To reinstate the Glass-Steagall Act (a banking reform passed
    in 1933 and partially repealed in 1980)*
Paid sick leave for all working Americans
Greater political transparency in general

Our conversation was serious but also light-hearted. One person suggested that universal care centers be established in former post offices, once the USPS folds. Another objected to full employment as a demand, saying that Americans already work too much. In the middle of our discussion, we debated why it was problematic to make a demand, how in order for a demand to be meaningful, one must have some power to leverage. Someone asked if we could demand that our list of demands be published in *Harper's*.

As we talked, people came up and joined our circle. It was not always clear who knew someone in the group and who was a stranger. One man sat down and told us that Wall Street was not the place we should be, that we should find the "nerve centers," the semi-secret non-governmental organizations that write laws. Meanwhile, protesters marched around the perimeter of the plaza chanting "Whose streets? Our streets!" We talked about what criteria made for good demands.

Someone had told us that the small groups would present their deliberations later in the evening, and eventually we decided that repealing the *Citizens United* Supreme Court decision was our best demand, since it would ostensibly create a more truly democratic political climate, through which our other demands could be met. We passed around a notebook and wrote down our emails so that we could continue to talk about how to repeal *Citizens United*. Then we were done.

A few days later, as I was trying to write this piece, I came across a passage in George Eliot: "For in general mortals have a great power of being astonished at the presence of an effect towards which they have done everything, and at the absence of an effect towards which they have done nothing but desire it." Was this us? Are we living and working in a city where in order to subsist, we must cooperate with the very injustices our demands were attempting to combat? A friend I saw that night asked derisively, "What were you protesting?" Then he laughed and added, "What weren't you protesting?" Is the whole thing stupid?

There is a temptation to say yes. Since Saturday, it has been harder for me to remain hesitant, to maintain my uncertainty about whether the people still occupying Liberty Plaza are succeeding, or could succeed, or even what success would be. We still don't know exactly what are the demands. One of the members of our group, in discussing the criteria for a good demand, noted that Americans like to "get something" out of a political action. Repeal, enact, ban. We want visible, measurable outcomes. But we have no Mubarak, no Qaddafi. We are the country that reelected Bush, that bailed out the banks, that has stalemates in Congress about paltry tax increases. Our partial joblessness and alienating democratic system may be very real, our reasons for congregating concrete, but the precise causes of our distress are still far off, the specific solutions perhaps further.

ELI SCHMITT, ASTRA TAYLOR & MARK GREIF

ONE NO, MANY YESES

MARINA SITRIN

I will begin with where I am right now—in New York. Though the beginning is before the Occupation and, before the before, much farther south. But first, New York.

The organizing group on the ground was the New York General Assembly. We began meeting during the summer of 2011. We sought to create the most horizontal and democratic space possible, using the assembly as our primary tool.

We discussed and debated the question of demands and what would define the movement, but we agreed not to use the framework of demands at all. So what are we about? Most of us believe that what is most important is to open space for conversations—for democracy—real, direct, and participatory democracy. Our only demand then would be to be left alone in our plazas, parks, schools, workplaces, and neighborhoods so as to meet one another, reflect together, and in assembly forms decide what our alternatives are. And from there, once we have opened up these democratic spaces, we can discuss what sort of demands we might have and who we believe might be able to meet these demands. Or, perhaps, once we have assemblies throughout the country, the issue of demands upon others will become mute. If there are enough of us, we may one day only make demands of ourselves.

For anyone who has participated in our nightly General Assembly in Liberty Plaza, you will likely have both felt totally inspired and not just a little confused about how it all works. Where do proposals come from? How do we come to agreement? Do people really listen to one another for hours at a time every night? Even when there are more than a thousand people? It might not appear very organized or clear, but, beneath the layers and layers of people, and the waves and waves of voices on the people's mic, is a web of networked organization. We organize in decentralized but connected working groups. Our working groups range in focus from the most concrete, such as food, medical, and legal, to things such as art, education, women's needs, and safer spaces. It is in these working groups that the day-to-day work of Occupy Wall Street takes place. Each working group, while autonomous, also brings

MARINA SITRIN

proposals to the larger group, the General Assembly, if the decision affects the entire body (e.g. negotiations with the mayor's office, or using money for bail, et cetera).

On any given day, education is organized, food is cooked and distributed to more than 1,000 people, legal advice is dispensed, video is livestreamed, and people's physical and mental health is attended to (we have a team of volunteer nurses and psychologists who are working with us). Translation into seven languages, including sign language, is available. The list of working groups and their responsibilities could fill a small book. And we have just begun.

Our communication between and among the working groups is not yet seamless, but we continue to work at it, and as we grow and change, our forms of organization necessarily change as well. New structures are constantly being explored, so that we may create the most open, participatory, and democratic space possible. We all strive to embody the alternative we wish to see in our day-to-day relationships.

On Newness and History

Many claim that what we are doing is new. This is both true and not true.

Our movements are not without precedent—quite the opposite. "One No, Many Yeses," for example, is a direct quotation from the Zapatistas of Chiapas, Mexico, who rose up in 1994 against NAFTA and what they called a death sentence for their country. The movement sparked the imaginations of millions of people around the world, and by the late 1990s other groups were emerging that also rejected the concept of hierarchical power, of looking to the state as the ultimate decision-maker, instead looking to one another. These sorts of groups ranged from the Direct Action Network in the US, which emerged as part of the 1999 Seattle protests against the WTO, to the social forums in Italy and many hundreds more around the world.

In 2001, the Argentine economy collapsed. The government had no solution. They froze people's bank accounts. In response, people took to the streets, first by the dozens, then hundreds, thousands, and then tens and hundreds of thousands. They did not go out with a political party or with any printed placard, but with pots and pans, banging them together, *cacerolando*. The one chant that came to the foreground in those days was "¡Que se vayan todos! ¡Que no quede ni uno solo!" (*They all must go! Not one should remain!*) And they did go: the country went through five governments in two weeks. At the same time, the people in the streets began to look around, to look to one another, to find and see one another for the first time. They created assemblies. People called it the most "natural" thing in the world, to seek out those harmed, just like you, and together begin to see if you can find solutions.

In Argentina, in those first days and weeks of the collapse, people formed hundreds of neighborhood assemblies. Workers took over their places of work and created horizontal assemblies to run them, moving to eliminate hierarchy, bosses, managers, and pay differentials. This new togetherness also took the form of a new term—*horizontalidad*. *Horizontalidad* is a social relationship that people at the time explained with a gesture of putting their hands out flat and moving them back and forth, showing a flat surface. Then, when asked to be more specific, people would say, well, it is not this—bringing their hands together to form a peak. People describe *horizontalidad* as a relationship that helps to create other things, but it is also a goal: the goal is to be more participatory and more horizontal by using the tools. It is about how one changes in the process of participation. People spoke of how this new relationship with their communities changed them, that the idea of "I" changed as it related to the "we," and this "we" changed again in relation to the "I."

Not a day goes by at Occupy Wall Street when I do not think about Argentina. And now I also think of the other occupations around the US. These assemblies are coming together and

MARINA SITRIN

creating alternatives to the crisis, opening discussion about what we want and how to achieve it. This is also a major characteristic of what has been taking place this past year around the globe, from Egypt to Spain. In Spain they say *¡Democracia Real Ya!* In Greece, they have even begun to use the ancient Greek: δημοκρατία. Demokratia. Soon, I hope, in our plazas and parks, our neighborhoods, schools, and workplaces, we will all be saying something similar: *Real Democracy!*

Photo by Stanley Rogouski

SCENES FROM AN OCCUPA-TION

ELI SCHMITT & ASTRA TAYLOR

Sunday, September 18

Astra:

I had a Zipcar tonight and was going into Manhattan, so I dropped off some provisions/supplies with the protesters. About the same number in the square, bedding down for a second night, and the scene was more raucous than yesterday, the occupiers more confident. "They read some books in college and now they think they know how to fix the world," one tired cop told some tourists as I walked by. A good many were assembling again as dusk fell, looking fervent, almost pious ("We need to talk about why we are here!") while others basically partied around them.

Monday, September 19

Eli:

I went back to Zuccotti Park on Monday around 11:30 PM. There were fifty people maybe, many of them sleeping or preparing to sleep. A kid playing guitar. Someone projecting images of Twitter onto a white screen. Hundreds of cardboard signs were laid out on the ground, lit by street lamps, waiting for protesters to take them up again. A chatty stranger from Virginia Beach told me he had just moved to New York. "Where do you live?" I asked. He gestured out at the park, at the topless men smoking hand-rolled cigarettes sitting in front of banks of computers set up on poured concrete flower beds. "I live here now. We're going to be here for a while."

Despite the repeated mentions of Tahrir Square and #globalrevolution on Twitter, the uprisings in the Middle East are probably not the best model for effecting change in America. But insofar as they constitute instances of political change instigated by groups of likeminded citizens, they are exciting to think about. It is exciting that people are upset and have claimed a public space as both a symbol of distress and a practical means of organizing. It is exciting that the protests and the occupation have persisted for over a week. It is possible, I think, without being starry-eyed or overeager, to

SCENES FROM AN OCCUPATION

be hopeful. And it is OK to be hesitant. It is OK to want to get something but also not be sure exactly how to get it, or even what it is. If we have not precisely enumerated our demands yet, at least we know that we have them. We would like to get something.

Photo by Jeremy Ayers

IT REALLY
IS ABOUT
THE 1%

DOUG HENWOOD &
THE CONGRESSIONAL
BUDGET OFFICE

Wow, that top one percent is doing really, really well, you'll not be surprised to hear. Everyone else, not so well.

The Congressional Budget Office is out with some new stats on trends in the distribution of income over the last three decades. Between 1979 and 2007, here's how various slices of the population did in real (inflation-adjusted) income growth after federal taxes:

top 1%   +275%
next 19%   +65%
middle 60% +40%
bottom 20% +18%

Or, in graphic form:

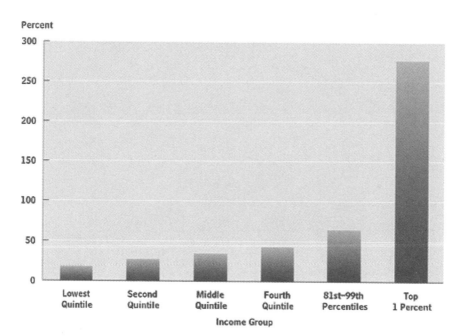

The stairstep pattern—the higher you go up the income ladder, the stronger the growth—is remarkable.

As a result of this vastly unequal growth, the share of after-tax income by population slice grew vastly more unequal:

top 1%	8% in 1979 to 17% in 2007, more than doubling
next 19%	35% in 1979, 36% in 2007, barely changed
middle 60%	50% in 1979, 43% in 2007, down 7 points
poorest 20%	down 2 points, from 7% to 5%

Or, in a picture:

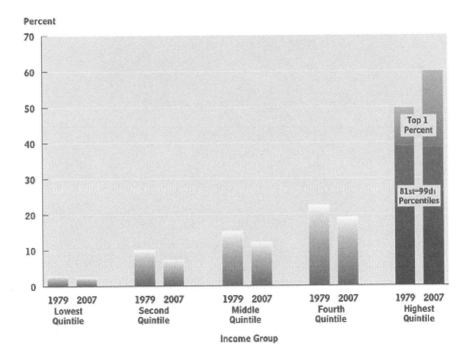

As of 2005, the share going to the top 20% surpassed the share going to the bottom 80%—though as the breakdown shows, most of this shift came from the very top. In 1979, the top 1% claimed about the same share as the bottom 20%; as of 2007, the top 1% hogged as much as the bottom 40%.

It really, really is 99 vs. 1.

Molly Crabapple, "Faces of Occupied Wall Street"

SCENES FROM AN OCCUPA- TION

ASTRA TAYLOR & MARK GREIF

Wednesday, September 21

Astra:

All these people are complaining that the occupiers don't have a clear agenda, a criticism that goes back to the Seattle WTO protest (and maybe beyond). Economic justice is the point. Doesn't their presence on Wall Street say that? There is plenty of "tax the rich" and "get corporate money out of politics" messaging going on. It's annoying that one topless lady can distract so many reporters, and also that 400 other people can't or won't just tell her to put a shirt on.

Friday, September 23

Astra:

Some of the people occupying Zuccotti Park are very young, and perhaps naïve in a lot of ways, but I'm happy they're doing it. That said, I'm always a bit irritated by the incessant emphasis on the youthfulness of the demonstrators, which is a way of infantilizing and dismissing them (silly kids, they'll grow up and get over this dumb protesting stuff!) and also lets older people off the hook. Shouldn't we all be out there, railing against the vampire squid? The fact is there are plenty of older people at Liberty Plaza, at least during the daytime hours—a good number of retirees mingling with the recent graduates. Our society, and the left especially, has this strange idea that young people are the revolutionary vanguard (in his famous "Letter to the New Left," C. Wright Mills made the case that youth had replaced the working class as the "historic agency"; Theodore Roszak calls this shift the "adolescentization of dissent"), but of course, being young, they don't have all the answers (not that old people do either, obviously). Related to this, I find the lack of historical knowledge (about past movements and effective strategies and tactics) and institutions through which to pass such wisdom down so depressing—each wave of kids reinvents the wheel, believes they've fashioned it for the first time, and then there it goes, off the rails. I hope a fraction of them dig in for the long haul

ASTRA TAYLOR & MARK CREIF

and build some sort of infrastructure so the next generation isn't left repeating this pattern.

Saturday, September 24

Astra:

After dinner I meandered down to Wall Street. There were maybe 400 or 500 people occupying the park, and the place was swarming with cops. They were on guard, menacing. Police vehicles kept racing around the periphery, sirens blaring. Dozens of buses and vans were parked around the corner, ready to be filled with detained protesters. I learned that a good number of demonstrators had been arrested earlier when they marched to Union Square. A video of two girls being penned in at Twelfth Street and University Avenue and maced at point-blank range by a zealous cop in a white shirt was making the online rounds. I watched it later that night, one victim falling to her knees, shrieking in pain, the other shaking with disbelief. An emergency General Assembly was called to discuss what to do in the event of a raid. One seemed imminent, though I couldn't really pay attention to what was being said since I kept checking to make sure I had a clear exit. A woman from the Upper East Side and I joke about starting a demonstration protesting the waste of taxpayer dollars on overtime for the cops.

Even though they had lost eighty people to the arrests and the police were in full intimidation mode, the plaza felt vital, emboldened. They've managed to stay a week, which is something. And they really appreciated the zucchini bread and the mango juice, so thanks for the donations.

I'd love it if a fraction of my friends who have presented sensible intellectual critiques of the action, or who have said, "They have a good message but they are the wrong people to spread it," showed up to Wall Street, since the implication is you want to see more people like yourselves down there.

Sunday, September 25

Mark:

Nine days is nothing to sneeze at. I know people keep complaining that the occupiers don't have a platform, but any real deliberative convention takes time, and these folks were strangers nine days ago. The idea of the occupation, to me, is to remind everyone that Wall Street belongs to the City of New York, the banks' money belongs to the people who have temporarily parked some of it with them (hoping they'll do some good with it), and the rules they play by ultimately come from us. Though I wish the NYPD didn't feel obliged to pen the protesters in, away from Wall Street, and I hope Burger King continues to be generous with its bathroom.

I made it to the General Assembly tonight. Weird for me, after a lifetime of internalizing the suspicion in universities and professional groups toward order, parliamentary procedure, and quick-running meetings, laughed away by saying, "Oh, since the sixties we've forgotten all that stuff!"—to see an efficient assembly managed by kids, democratically, inclusively, and good-humoredly. I wish *n+1* meetings ran like this. The left knows more than we think it does, as always. Noam Chomsky had sent an email. It was predictably long-winded; I wished people would make the "get to your point" sign. I was sitting close to the aisle of waiting speakers and was surprised to watch participants I assumed knew each other well—since they were working together smoothly—whisper to ask each other's names. They're the most easygoing bunch I've seen at a protest. Very gentle and not rattled by disruptors. Presumably that's the confidence of nine days. Also the multiple confrontations that they've won nonviolently. The arrestees—including the man thrown to the ground and jailed for stopping to address a Chase Bank branch about its foreclosure on his parents' house—came back and described the holding cells. The mix of protesters includes a core that stays overnight, fair-weather visitors (like me), older activists, hobos, and people who read as "students" of all different ages. The drum circle was not intolerable.

ASTRA TAYLOR & MARK CREIF

LETTERS OF RESIG- NATION FROM THE AMERICAN DREAM

MARCO ROTH

A web page, white and red letters against a black background, a scrollable gallery of faces, most of them almost entirely hidden by handwritten notes in a variety of colors and formats. One, the quarter face of a bald, bearded white man, holding a yellow legal pad, where he's written in block print capitals, "I work 3 jobs, none which provide health insurance. My son is on Medicaid. We are on W.I.C. We're one paycheck from disaster. I am the 99%." Another, showing only a young woman's fingers gripping her note:

> *I graduated college a year ago and have a job as a journalist. I am lucky. Every time we have a staff meeting someone is laid off. My entire office is struggling; professionals making less than 30K a year. I am scared everyday that I will lose my job and be stuck with 50K in student loans that won't be paid off until I am 40. After loan payments and car insurance I am left with only money for gas. I am extremely lucky, it could be worse, at least I can live with my parents for a while. I am the 99 percent.*

And so it goes down the scroll, and for pages and pages: returning veterans without jobs and with variously crippling disabilities; a would-be member of the professional class, "I have three master's degrees, no job, and over 80,000 in student debt"; a woman who says she and her husband are afraid to have children because "they will be part of the 99%"; another woman who writes her own epitaph in the last line of her testimony: "First in my family to go to college. Built a wonderful international career in nonprofits. Now I'm unable to get a cashier job at the zoo because chronic depression, unemployment, and lack of access to medical care ruined my credit score. I played by the rules." There are teachers, kids afraid to go to college, the children of immigrants who realize they will have worse lives than their parents, grandparents worried about their grandchildren and their own retirements. In most of the photographs, faces are either partially hidden or downcast, in attitudes of shame; a few, mostly the young-est, look out defiantly. It cannot go on. It goes on.

The website, an open blog, or tumblr, called "We Are the 99 Percent" is one of the few and more remarkable documents to emerge from the Occupy Wall Strcct movement. The diversity of the stories and faces on display provides a pretty definitive rebuttal to anyone still naïve or malicious enough to claim that the movement is composed exclusively of hippies, anarchists, and other phantasms of the 1960s New Left conjured by CNN, National Review Online, and the editors of the *New Republic*. The tumblr provides a portrait in aggregate of the emerging majority of Americans: indebted, often over-educated for the few jobs and salaries available to them, stripped of dignity, tormented by anxieties over how to care for themselves and their families, laid off from jobs, non-unionized, clinging pre-cariously to an idea of middle-classness that seems more and more to be a chimera of the past. Never mind democracy, this is what a "lost decade" looks like. Behold the human, subjec-tive correlatives of what Paul Krugman, Joseph Stiglitz, and

From wearethe99percent.tumblr.com

other honorable economists were warning about when they described the effects of life in a chronic liquidity trap, when businesses won't invest in labor and the government fails to stimulate the economy.

Politically and culturally, however, "We Are the 99 Percent" offers a more ambiguous series of messages. The nation and society that can produce this kind of document is undoubtedly in the throes of a nasty transformation. A historically minded reader will be reminded of the few testimonies by English independent hand-loom weavers at the end of the eighteenth century, unearthed by E. P. Thompson in his *Making of the English Working Class*. Driven off the land into wage and debt slavery to large textile manufacturers in Manchester and elsewhere, after the advent of the power loom, the weavers, a mostly literate group, told their stories in letters to their families and magistrates, or recorded them in popular ballads. It was a time when, as Wordsworth put it in a poem about the fate of one such weaving family, "many rich sunk down as in a dream among the poor,/ and of the poor did many cease to be,/ and their place knew them not." For all the pathos of the plight of the weavers, they are now mostly remembered as a footnote to the larger movements of modernity and industrialization of which they were victims. The creation of an archive or memorial, even in real time, does not, by itself, constitute resistance, and it might be the case that the 99 percenters recorded on the tumblr will be viewed by future historians as the necessary fallen of the age of post-industrialization, the great adjustment, or whatever name, probably in Chinese or Brazilian Portuguese, they give our present moment of economic and social realignment.

At the same time, there is a certain limited but important power behind all these displays of futility: By writing "I am the 99%" or in some cases "We are the 99%" at the end of their litanies, the individuals who have chosen to post their post-industrial miseries on the web are doing something that Americans of recent generations have been averse to doing. They are actually creating class consciousness, for themselves

MARCO ROTH

and those around them. It's not just a gesture, but a speech act in the same way, for instance, as saying that you accept Jesus Christ as your savior is enough to make you a Christian among certain born-again churches. When an individual chooses to follow the instructions of wearethe99percent.tumblr.com—

Let us know who you are. Take a picture of yourself holding a sign that describes your situation—for example, "I am a student with $25,000 in debt," or "I needed surgery and my first thought wasn't if I was going to be okay, it was how I'd afford it." Below that, write "I am the 99 percent."

—he or she writes a letter of resignation from the American Dream and pledges allegiance to the 99 percent movement, the goals of which remain as yet undefined even as it builds strength with every person who, as the tumblr puts it, "gets known."

The voluntary humility of these gestures is subtly reinforced by an association, one that will immediately spring to the mind of anyone who has lived in a major American city, between these handwritten accounts of personal troubles and the signs often carried by the homeless: "HIV Positive, No Insurance, Please Help," "Homeless Vietnam Vet," "Published Poet: New York Times, Amsterdam News, etc. Now sells his poems directly to you!" Intended or accidental element of style, this identification of the Occupy movement and the urban homeless and panhandlers emerges as one of the most uncanny and powerfully disturbing aspects of the current protests. Just as the early communists heralded the proletariat as the repository of potential revolutionary consciousness, so OWS holds up the homeless as the privileged figure of contemporary American post-capitalist life. This elevation of homelessness by reducing everyone outside the one percent of über-capitalists to their ranks occurs at more than the level of signage. The reclamation of the semi-public sphere being carried out in Zuccotti Park and elsewhere in America is, it turns out, of immediate practical benefit to the permanently urban homeless who may shortly be able to begin claiming the political dignity of occupation for themselves, not to mention access to the unofficial support network of soup kitchens, medical tents, libraries, and legal advice set up by the occupiers.

On the other hand, as with all solidarity politics, mostly practiced in Europe, "We are all German Jews," "We are all illegal immigrants," and, briefly, after 9/11, "We are all Americans," "We are all homeless" clashes against certain existing realities, as when an actual homeless man interrupted a meeting of the Education working group at Occupy Philadelphia to ask for money. The consternation on the faces of the occupiers was visible, and when the man lay down just outside the circle, on the concrete, the group's coordinator, a young woman who flashed with the magnetizing beauty that seems to attach to so many who assumed leading roles in OWS, immediately sat down next to him, futilely attempting to persuade him to move, while the meeting dissolved into chaos. At that moment, however, she was no longer acting in ruthless solidarity ("We're out here with you, brother," as one guy called out, his hands never moving from his pockets), but in more old-fashioned sympathy. She could afford to take time off from the revolution, she thought, because whatever percentage she was, she had resources that the homeless guy did not have. These habits do not get unlearned overnight or even over several nights, and it might not turn out very well if we did thoroughly unlearn them.

As a slogan, it's hard to get less individualistic than "I am the 99%." Yet the personal narratives of American suffering have a hard time staying out of people's testimonies: I've read about child abuse and marital breakups. I've performed amateur graphology to see if the guy who says he has three doctorates might be exaggerating. At a certain point, I simply ran aground against the conundrum encapsulated by the "banks got bailed out, we got sold out" chant. Is OWS a movement calling for the people to be bailed out too, or a movement of noble anger against the corporate welfare state we've been living in? Or is it, in fact, an actual liberation movement, aimed largely at reclaiming the freedom of the streets for popular assembly, against tourism and a managed public sphere? Is this, in fact, the largest homeless rights movement on the planet?

Having looked at "We Are the 99 Percent" for pages and pages, I was suddenly overcome with an odd desire to see those iconic Walker Evans photographs of the Depression-era South in *Let Us Now Praise Famous Men*. Those photos, so austere, so pure, are seared into the cultural memory of a certain American generation: the cool-eyed stare of the young woman, framed against the clapboard side of a house, her mouth in a thin, crooked almost-smile that doesn't quite prevent us from noticing the cheeks sunken from malnourishment and early loss of teeth, the barefoot, tow-headed children on their rickety porches, amid the cast-down farm tools, a pair of worn and dusty boots. Part of a WPA project that aimed to call attention to the depth of rural American poverty, Evans's photographs perversely ended up memorializing and ennobling the hardness of the lives that the government he worked for wanted to ameliorate. Through the very stoicism that came out on camera and in James Agee's accompanying text, his subjects came to signify the virtuous poor who deserved "a hand up, not a handout," although they mostly got food stamps. Those images were made to convince a public of outsiders, and that is the very thing that makes the suffering they display so easy on the eye, all these generations later. I wanted some old-time stoicism that I could project my emotions on, like the good liberal I stubbornly remain, even though I know that, in politics, no silence goes unpunished. What I wanted from OWS, too, as an outsider, was greater dignity, even while knowing that they wouldn't be so indignant if America hadn't lost all its own long ago. "We Are the 99 Percent" is more an internal document of the movement than an external one. It doesn't want your sympathy, although many of the stories are written in a language designed to evoke sympathy. It's an invitation to identify, to join the party and accept the consequences of acknowledging that, in fact, we are the 99 percent.

David Kearns, "Occupation Sketchbook"

SCENES FROM AN OCCUPA- TION

ELIZABETH GUMPORT

Thursday, September 29

Elizabeth:

I went back to Zuccotti Park last night for the first time since the 17th. Michael Moore was there, reporting for MSNBC from the corner of Liberty Street and Trinity Place. A crowd gathered around him; "down in front," people called out, and everyone sat down. Then most of them stood back up. A shot of Michael Moore sitting in a director's chair, in a dark, possibly empty park, surrounded by a couple of security guards: apparently this does not make for good television. We're live, someone said, and a boy standing behind Moore waved at the camera. People held their phones up the air and took pictures, like they do at concerts.

Meanwhile, on the other side of the park, the General Assembly was in session. The group here was much larger than the one gathered around Moore, but it didn't feel like a crowd—people were calm, attentive, at ease. A lot of them were sitting down. In order to be heard, speakers relied on "human microphones": they'd say a few words, then pause while the group repeated the phrase. After an explanation of the assembly process for the sake of any newcomers, the working groups delivered their reports. A comfort team representative requested sweatshirts, sweatpants, and socks. Justin from Community Relations told everyone, "You look so beautiful tonight." "You look so beautiful tonight," everyone repeated, and they were right. They did look very beautiful. Maybe only someone as ignorant of strategy—of history—as I am would be impressed by this. But people—the ones who figured out how to do these things, the ones doing them now—are impressive! There was an announcement: the night before, someone named Sergio had asked for a translator. A translator had been found and was present at the Assembly. If Sergio was there—and he was! There was Sergio, joyful, emerging from the circle. Someone else read a letter from the Canadian Union of Postal Workers, thanking the occupiers for rallying in solidarity with New York City postal employees on Tuesday.

Later, I dropped off the supplies I'd brought—cough drops, Cold-Eeze, tampons—with a protester manning the medical station. He'd come from California and has been there since the beginning. The first night, he said, about sixty people camped out; tonight he estimated it would be six hundred. Two recent arrivals had some questions for him: where did people go to use the bathroom? (McDonald's—the nearby Burger King won't even serve protesters anymore, never mind let them use the restroom.) Was it OK to leave their bags out? (Pretty much, just be sure to put your camera or whatever in a case.) And then: what were they doing? Or going to do next— or what—he wasn't quite sure how to put it, but the veteran occupier nodded understandingly. It was the same implicit, atmospheric question that had been asked when I joined my friends in the park on the 17th, the first day of the protest. We sat, talked, proposed demands, and left before dusk—not a bad way to spend an afternoon. But it had been summer then, and it was fall now, and night: a new season, a change in the air. Something had been affirmed, and now there was a greater sense of opportunity—and also, perhaps, responsibility. The question might have been the same, but now, twelve days later, maybe the answer was—or could be, or should be— different. (Which doesn't mean rushed: it takes time to take things seriously.)

Across the plaza, the General Assembly was still going on. Russell Simmons briefly addressed the crowd, followed by a woman who knew how to crochet and proposed starting a group to make hats, scarves, and gloves. It was, she said, going to get cold soon. It was already raining, and I left. On the train home, I opened the book I'd brought with me and found in it the words for what it was I'd felt in the park: "The present winter is worth an age, if rightly employed."

STANDING
UP

MANISSA MAHARAWAL

I first went down to Occupy Wall Street almost a week after it had started. I hadn't gone down earlier because, like many of my brown friends, I was wary of what I had heard or just intuited that it was mostly a young white male scene.

But after hearing about the arrests and police brutality on Saturday and after hearing that thousands of people had turned up for their march, I decided to see for myself. A friend and I biked over the Brooklyn Bridge around noon, dodging the tourists and cars on Chambers Street. We ended up at Ground Zero. For a moment we felt lost. The landscape was strange. We were in the shadow of half-built buildings. They glittered and twisted into the sky. But they also seemed so naked: rust-colored steel poking out of their tops, their sides, their guts spilling out for all to see. Finally we got to Liberty Plaza. At first it seemed so unassuming; we didn't entirely know what to do. We wandered around. We made posters and laid them on the ground. I didn't know anyone down there. Not one person.

There were a lot of young white kids. But there weren't only young white kids. There were older people, there were mothers with kids, and there were a lot more people of color than I expected. We sat on the stairs and watched everyone mill around us. There was the usual protest feeling of people moving around in different directions, not sure what to do, but within this there was also order: a food table, a library, a busy media area. I watched as a man carefully changed each piece of his clothing, folding his shirt, his socks, his pants, and placing them carefully under a tarp. I used the bathroom at the McDonald's up Broadway and there were two booths of people from the protest carrying out meetings, eating food from Liberty Plaza, sipping water out of water bottles, their laptops out. They were conspicuous yet also just part of the normal Financial District hustle and bustle.

I stayed for a few hours, impressed and energized by what I saw: people seemed to be taking care of each other. There seemed to be a general feeling of solidarity and it was less disorganized than I expected. The whole thing was bizarre:

confused tourists not knowing what was going on; police officers lining the perimeter; the mixture of young white kids with dreadlocks, anarchist punks, mainstream-looking college kids. But also the awesome black woman who was organizing the food station, the older man who walked around with his peace sign who stopped to talk to everyone. A young black man named Chris from New Jersey who told me he had been there all week and he was tired but that he had come not knowing anyone, had made friends, and now he didn't want to leave.

When I left, walking my bike back through the streets of the Financial District, fighting the crowds of tourists and men in suits, I felt something pulling me back to that space. I started telling my friends to go down there and check it out. I started telling people that it was a pretty awesome thing, that just having a space to have these conversations mattered, that it was more diverse than I expected. And I went back.

Later I attended my first General Assembly. Seeing 300 people using the consensus method was powerful. We consensed on using donations to bail out the people who had been arrested. I was impressed that such a large group made a financial decision in a relatively painless way. After the General Assembly that night there was both a talent show on one side of the plaza ("This is what a talent show looks like!") and an Anti-Patriarchy working group meeting (which became the Safer Spaces working group) on the other. In some ways the juxtaposition of both these events happening at once is emblematic of one of the splits at the park: talent shows across the square from anti-patriarchy meetings, an announcement that someone has lost their phone. Maybe this is how movements need to maintain themselves, through a recognition that political change is also fundamentally about everyday life and that everyday life needs to encompass all of this: There needs to be a space for a talent show across from an anti-patriarchy meeting, there needs to be a food table and medics, a library, and everyone needs to stop for a second and look around for someone's phone.

MANISSA MAHARAWAL

I went to the anti-patriarchy meeting because even though I was impressed by the General Assembly and its process, I also noticed that it was mostly white men who were in charge of the committees and making announcements, and that I had only seen one woman of color get up in front of everyone and talk. A lot was said at the anti-patriarchy meeting about the ways in which the space of the occupation was a safe space and ways it was not. Women talked about feeling uncomfortable in the drum circle because of men dancing up on them and how to change this, about how to feel safe sleeping out in the open with a lot of men they didn't know, and about not assuming gender pronouns and asking people which pronouns they would prefer.

The next night I showed up at Occupy Wall Street with a group that had just attended a South Asians for Justice meeting, and the GA was in session. People were passing around the Declaration of the Occupation of Wall Street, which I had heard read the night before. I hadn't realized that it was going to be finalized as THE declaration of the movement right then and there. When I heard it the night before with my friend Sonny, we noted that a line about the eradication of race, class, and gender divisions seemed strange. Did they really think these problems were behind us? But Sonny and I had shrugged it off as the ramblings of one of the many working groups at Occupy Wall Street.

Now we realized that this was actually a really important document, that it was going to be sent into the world and read by thousands of people. And that if we let it go into the world the way it was, it would mean that people like me would shrug this movement off. It would keep people like me and my friends and my community from joining this movement. So this was urgent. This movement was about to send a document into the world about who and what it was that included a line that erased the memory of all power relations and ignored decades of oppression. I didn't want to walk away from this. I couldn't walk away. And that night I was with people who also couldn't walk away. Our contingent did not back down. We did not back down when we were told, the first time that my friend Hena spoke, that our concerns could be emailed and didn't need to be dealt with then; we didn't back down when we were told that a second time; and we didn't back down when we were told that to "block" the declaration from going forward was a serious serious thing to do. I knew it was a serious thing to do, we all knew it was a serious thing to do, and that is why we did it.

I have never blocked something before. And the only reason I was able to do so was because there were five of us standing together and because Hena had already put herself out there and started shouting "mic check" until they paid attention. And the only reason that I could speak out in that moment was because I felt so urgently that this was something that needed to be said. There is something intense about speaking in front of hundreds of people, but there is something even more intense about speaking in front of hundreds of people with whom you feel aligned and you are saying something that they do not want to hear. And then it is even more intense when that crowd is repeating everything you say, which is the way the General Assemblies or any announcements at Occupy Wall Street work. But hearing yourself in an echo chamber means that you make sure your words mean something, because they are being said back to you as you say them. And so when we finally got everyone's attention I carefully explained the issue. We wanted a small change in language, a change representative of a larger ethical concern: to act like oppression is a thing of the past, we argued, is wrong.

They accepted our change and we withdrew our block. They said, "Find us after and we will go through it." And then it was over and everyone began to disperse.

After the meeting we found a man who had helped write the document and told him that he needed to change or take out the first line of the declaration: "As one people, formerly divided by the color of our skin, gender, sexual orientation, religion, or lack thereof, political party and cultural background,

MANISSA MAHARAWAL

we acknowledge the reality: that there is only one race, the human race ..."

But it's "scientifically true," he told us. There was only one race. Were we advocating for there being different races?

No, we said. Of course we weren't. What we were trying to say was that by beginning a document that was going to be the declaration of Occupy Wall Street in a way that sounded as if racism, classism, religious oppression, patriarchy, homophobia and trans-phobia no longer existed, in a way that sounded as if this movement didn't need to take on the history and legacy of oppression or address the way these things play out within the movement and outside of it, was naïve and alienating to people who felt these things on a daily basis. That in fact *we* felt some of these things on a daily basis. That in order for this movement to be inclusive it needed to acknowledge these realities and find creative ways to work through them instead of ignoring them.

And so, there in that circle, on that street corner, we did a crash course on white privilege, structural racism, and oppression. We did a course on history and the Declaration of Independence and colonialism and slavery. And let me tell

STANDING UP

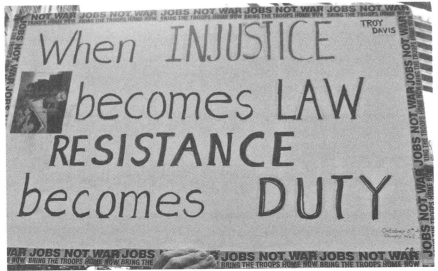

Photo by Jeremy Ayers

you what it feels like to stand in front of a white man and explain privilege to him. It hurts. It makes you tired. Sometimes it makes you want to cry. Sometimes it is exhilarating. Every single time it is hard.

But people listened. We had to fight for it, but it felt worth it. It felt worth it to sit down on a street corner in the Financial District at 11:30 PM on a Thursday night, after working all day long and argue for changing the first line of Occupy Wall Street's official Declaration of the Occupation of New York City. It felt worth it not only because we got the line changed but also because standing there, speaking up—carefully and slowly spelling out that I experience the world differently from him, that this was not about him being personally racist but about relations of power, that he urgently needed to listen and believe me about this—felt like a victory for the movement on its own.

The line was removed. We sat down and re-wrote the opening of the Declaration, and it has been published with our re-write. And when we walked away, I felt like something important had just happened, that we had just pushed the movement a little bit closer to the movement I would like to see, one that takes into account historical and current inequalities, oppressions, racisms, relations of power, one that doesn't just reinforce privilege but confronts it head on.

Later that night I biked home over the Brooklyn Bridge and I somehow felt like, just maybe, at least in that moment, the world belonged to me as well as to everyone dear to me and everyone who needed and wanted more from the world. I somehow felt like maybe the world could be all of ours.

MANISSA MAHARAWAL

SCENES FROM AN OCCUPA- TION

SARAH RESNICK, KEITH GESSEN & SARAH LEONARD

Saturday, October 1

Sarah Resnick, Sent 10/1/2011 @ 1:50 PM
Hey, trains all fucked up. I don't know that I could get to wall street in time for march but I'm up for meeting down there later this afternoon. Also, I think there is a big labor march on wednesday organized by Twu.

XXXX XXXX, Sent 10/1/2011 @ 3:18 PM
March ending on Bkln side of bridge

XXXX XXXX, Sent 10/1/2011 @ 4:20 PM
Taken every lane of Bkln bridge

Sarah Resnick, Sent 10/1/2011 @ 4:23 PM
That's amazing. I am on the 7 train. Got stuck at book fair with no umbrella.

XXXX XXXX, Sent 10/1/2011 @ 4:39 PM
Cops have penned us in the middle of the bridge. Maybe letting us leave single file but unclear.

XXXX XXXX, Sent 10/1/2011 @ 5:09 PM
Might get arrested in a bit. Cops are slowly moving people off bridge.

Sarah Resnick, Sent 10/1/2011 @ 5:19 PM
Really? What a waste of city resources. Keep me posted.

Sarah Resnick, Sent 10/1/2011 @ 6:39 PM
Did you make it out okay?

Sarah Resnick, Sent 10/1/2011 @ 9:17 PM
Okay, assuming you were arrested. If so, call 212 679 6018 when you out. The NLG. They are providing legal support/criminal defense.

XXXX XXXX, Sent 10/2/2011 @ 2:43 AM
I'm out.

David Kearns, "Occupation Sketchbook"

Sarah R:

A friend in the frontlines of Saturday's march told me that the Brooklyn Bridge occupation was, in fact, a purposeful act. Thus far, media accounts of that afternoon had put forward conflicting information, and the story circulating through my

Facebook network and in many left-sympathetic outlets was that police seemingly directed protesters onto the bridge only to net them in and arrest them moments later—entrapment! But my friend disputed this account, offering a very different perspective. Once the congestion of the pedestrian walkways forced protesters to spill over on the roadway, he told me, a group toward the front launched into a refrain: "Take the bridge! Take the bridge!" Assured they had the support of the hundreds of protesters behind them—all of whom were now chanting in unison—they locked arms to lead a slow and purposeful advance on the police line. At first, the police admonished the protesters, demanding they redirect onto the walkways; but, vastly outnumbered, they capitulated, yielding to the advancing marchers.

Those who instigated the bridge seizure were in fact dismayed by the media portrayal. Why ascribe what is otherwise a victory for OWS—that is, remarkable evidence of the strength and power of the masses united—to the rancor of the police? Why recast a moment of transcendence as one of dupery and oppression?

Tuesday, October 4

Keith:

There must have been ten thousand people today in Foley Square. It took your breath away. All those courthouses, five of them—including the one on whose steps Corleone enforcer Al Neri, dressed as a police officer, shot Barzini in *The Godfather*, on the day Michael exacted revenge against the heads of the Five Families—usually give the square a desolate look, like you've suddenly been dropped into Washington, D.C. But with all these people on it, it felt . . . European. There were plenty of middle-aged union workers, as the press would later point out; there were representatives of numerous community organizations from across the city, including the housing projects near where I live, in Brooklyn; but there were also plenty of the sort of interesting-looking, serious-looking, but also, you

SARAH RESNICK, KEITH GESSEN & SARAH LEONARD

secretly suspect, totally frivolous people more or less your age that you see walking around the city, never knowing who they are. Comrades, it turns out.

Sarah L:

The media have begun to ask hungrily, "What's next?" It's often an apprehensive question directed at a quasi-movement that has managed to escalate in size and tension every week. The 700 arrests on the Brooklyn Bridge on Saturday drew attention way beyond the best organized union march. Police brutality continues to trigger coverage, and by blockading Wall Street on Wednesday after the huge meeting at Foley Square, they set up another site of confrontation.

The most spectacular show of force came when a large group decided to march away from Wall Street, and wind back toward it, later Wednesday night. "Whose streets? Our streets!" we shouted as the police corralled us onto the sidewalk. We walked through dark streets on narrow sidewalks, hemmed in by a line of motorcycle cops so close together that sometimes they bumped wheels. More officers ran alongside. And on our other side, officers stood in doorways holding nightsticks. "Police! Join us! They want your pensions too!" There were helicopters. Little wildcat marches reportedly made their way through the streets as well, confronting the police as they sought an approach to Wall Street.

It's starting to look like there is a critical mass of people ready to make headlines out of taxpayer-funded cops keeping New Yorkers from directly protesting the banks that they bailed out.

SCENES FROM AN OCCUPATION

THE THEOLOGY OF CONSEN- SUS

L. A. KAUFFMAN

From the start, Occupy Wall Street has embraced consensus decision-making, a process in which groups come to agreement without voting. Instead of voting up or down on a controversial proposal, groups that make decisions by consensus work to refine it until everyone finds it acceptable. A primer on the NYC General Assembly website explains, "Consensus is a creative thinking process: When we vote, we decide between two alternatives. With consensus, we take an issue, hear the range of enthusiasm, ideas and concerns about it, and synthesize a proposal that best serves everybody's vision."

Consensus has been adopted by a wide array of social movements over the last thirty-five years, and proponents make broad claims for it. They argue that it is intrinsically more democratic than other methods and that it fosters radical transformation, both within movements and in their relations with the wider world. As described in the handbook of an Earth Day 1990 action to shut down Wall Street, which included a blockade of the entrances to the stock exchange and led to some 200 arrests, "Consensus at its best offers a cooperative model of reaching group unity, an essential step in creating a culture that values cooperation over competition."

Few know the origins of the process, though they shed an interesting and surprising light on its workings. Consensus decision-making first entered the world of grassroots activism in the summer of 1976, when a group of activists calling themselves the Clamshell Alliance began a direct action campaign against the planned Seabrook Nuclear Plant.

Many activists at the time were well aware of what feminist writer Jo Freeman famously called "the tyranny of structurelessness." The tendency in some early 1970s movements to abandon all structure in the name of spontaneity and informality had proven to be not just unworkable but undemocratic. Decisions still happened, but without an agreed-upon process, there was no accountability.

The organizers of "the Clam," as it was often called, were eager to find a process that could prevent the pitfalls of structurelessness without resorting to hierarchy. Two staff people from the American Friends Service Committee, the long-standing and widely admired peace and justice organization affiliated with the Society of Friends, or Quakers, suggested consensus.

As historian A. Paul Hare wrote, "For over 300 years the members of the Society of Friends (Quakers) have been making group decisions without voting. Their method is to find a 'sense of the meeting' which represents a consensus of those involved. Ideally this consensus is not simply 'unanimity,' or an opinion on which all members happen to agree, but a 'unity': a higher truth which grows from the consideration of divergent opinions and unites them all."

The process, adherents believe, is in effect a manifestation of the divine. A 1943 "Guide to Quaker Practice" explained, "The principle of corporate guidance, according to which the Spirit can inspire the group as a whole, is central. Since there is but one Truth, its Spirit, if followed, will produce unity."

Quakers do not, as a rule, proselytize their faith, and the two AFSC organizers working on the Seabrook anti-nuclear campaign were no exception. They introduced the decision-making method without any theological content. As one of

L. A. KAUFFMAN

Photo by Stanley Rogouski

48

the activists, Sukie Rice, told me in a 2002 interview, "Friends consider [consensus] a waiting upon the Spirit, that you pray that you will do God's will, and that wasn't there in the Clam. The Clam used it as a decision-making process that was consistent with nonviolence."

Rice continued, "[The activists of the Clam] had no idea that Clamshell would be the prototype for all the other groups that took off from there, they had no inkling of that." But indeed it was. After the Clam, consensus became the accepted decision-making process among many segments of the activist left, especially those that embraced direct action as central to their strategy, up to and including today's Occupy movements. And though Rice and her colleague were careful to exclude any explicit theology from their trainings on consensus, something of that religious origin arguably adheres to it up to the present day.

Perhaps it's something about the reverence with which consensus is sometimes discussed in activist circles, leaving those who find it unwieldy to feel like apostates. Perhaps it's the assumption embedded in the process that division results from differing views (which can be reconciled) rather than competing interests (which often cannot).

Perhaps it's the way it sometimes seems to be, well, an article of faith that consensus is intrinsically more democratic and more radical than other forms of decision-making.

Consensus process has considerable virtues, but it also has flaws. It favors those with lots of time to spend in meetings. Unless practiced with unusual skill, it can lavish excessive attention on the stubborn or disruptive. Occupy Wall Street has opened up for questioning so much that was previously taken as given. May it do the same with its own methods.

THE THEOLOGY OF CONSENSUS

Dan Archer, "Occupied Oakland"

SCENES FROM AN OCCUPA- TION

KEITH GESSEN, ASTRA TAYLOR & SARAH RESNICK

KEITH GESSEN, ASTRA TAYLOR & SARAH RESNICK

Wednesday, October 5

Keith:

On the day Talib Kweli did a surprise performance at the GA, I had to leave early in search of a bathroom. I walked around the park, thinking I might ask someone, and eventually concluded that there was no one to ask. Each man for himself. For a moment, the upstairs seating area at Steve's Pizza looked promising, until I saw, as I walked toward it, two cops ushering protesters out. Next door was the Burger King. Nonchalantly I walked up to the second floor. They had stationed an employee there. He asked, was I headed for the restroom? Because then I had to be a customer. I headed back outside.

Eventually I found myself at Century 21, the giant designer discount store. There was a bathroom in the basement. I had thought the park was crowded, but Century 21, too, was full. European tourists snatched up discounted wallets, belts, sunglasses. What an adventure it had been, just to take a leak.

Friday, October 7

Astra:

A young man, impersonating a carnival barker, invited me to step right up and write down how much I was worth to the banks. "How much money do you owe?" he shouted. "Come and tell us how valuable you really are to the one percent." A small group of us gathered round, waiting for a turn to confess our debt on giant sheets of white paper. $42,000, I wrote, my stomach sinking as I faced the number I usually keep at bay, since dwelling on it makes me panic. Damn student loans. I handed the marker to the girl behind me, who looked to be in her early twenties. Next to her name she wrote $120,000.

Since the sixties, the usual smear against protesters is that they are lazy hippies who should get a job, or privileged rich kids who don't have to work and therefore don't have a right to speak for the common person. They're hippies, weirdos, slackers. In 2011 these slurs don't have as much sway as they once did. Back then higher education was virtually free, unemployment was low, and minimum wage, adjusted for inflation, was at a record high. Meanwhile, the draft deferment that college enrollment granted deepened class antagonisms. Today the cost of university has skyrocketed, while it has been estimated that 85 percent of young people will have to move back home after graduating from college, weighed down by loans they may not ever be able to pay back. Makes me wonder: Would most people rather go back and live with mom and dad or camp somewhere like Zuccotti Park?

Sarah R:

I arrived late to the GA. At the mic, a man brought forward a proposal for a new working group: the Résumé group. "There are several of us here who are unemployed," he said. "I'd like to propose a group to support those of us in need of work as we develop and even distribute our résumés." Several palms raised, fingers waving—a show of support. The woman to my right was over sixty and—judging from her question—in attendance for the first time. "What's that irritating noise?" she asked me. "Is that a police tactic of disruption? Are they trying to make it difficult for us to hear each other?" She was, of course, referring to the clamor of the drum circle, which was, from our vantage, entirely out of sight. Their ceaseless revelry had quickly become a point of contention among protesters; the din was so deafening that night that it may as well have been sonic weaponry. I experienced a moment of paranoia: Was it possible the police were behind the drum circle, undercover cops unleashing their sacred masculine? Without legal recourse to evict the park's new residents, a more brilliant plan couldn't have been devised: Drive everyone to irritable madness!

During announcements, a man who claimed to carry a message from the Egyptian revolution spoke to the GA: "Choose your leaders now!" he cried. "Choose one demand now or your movement is lost!" The human mic ceased amplification, drowned by audible disapproval. This "leaderless resistance movement with people of many political persuasions," as it calls itself, was not about to concede autonomy or participatory democracy or any of its founding tenets—not yet at least.

A facilitator took charge—we were moving on to the agenda. "Tonight there is one item to discuss: transparency." The movement is growing larger, we were told, and many important decisions are happening in groups outside the GA. The speaker acknowledged that he too was sometimes part of these behind-the-scenes decision-making bodies. But we were being asked—how might they (we?) foster a space of communicative openness and direct accountability? How could the movement sustain transparency even as it grew? We would move into temporary breakout groups to discuss and propose solutions. The assignment contained what I saw as a peculiar irony: Please tell those of us acting sub rosa how to better inform you about that which you don't know you aren't being informed. What "unknown unknowns" were we being asked to account for?

That there was an issue of transparency was not news to me. The GA was not, as I understood it, where core planning was being formulated, where key decisions were being passed—at least not anymore, not now that the numbers were so considerable. Partly this was gleaned from talking to people embedded deep in the organization of OWS—already there were rumors of backroom dealings with various NGOs and unions. But it was also common sense. Not every group with an ideological stake in the movement would take part in its manifest structure of openness and participation. As anyone with a secret knows, withholding information is a strategic decision. Where risk is involved, trust can subsist only among a few. Covertness is, at times, a necessity, and in some instances—like initial plans for future occupations—the movement may depend on it.

I wanted to stay for the discussion, but I was to meet a friend. I resolved to read the minutes later online, only to find that, at least as of this writing, they've still not been posted.

DRUMMING
IN
CIRCLES

MARK GREIF

Where do drum circles come from? If ever there were a topic you'd expect graduate students in anthropology to write dissertations on, this would be it. It combines all the favorite elements of contemporary ethnography: a genuinely popular practice that bubbles up within tiny communities that still constitute themselves by name and often geographical affiliation (Venice Beach Drum Circle, Congo Square Drum Circle [in Prospect Park], Earth Drum Council) and self-regulate like utopian scale-models of the larger society. A partly imaginary, partly historic attempt to live out suppressed anti-colonial traditions of Native American spirituality and survival and the African diaspora in the Americas and Caribbean. Contemporary intermingling of Deadheads and transplanted Californians, African-American b-boys, African immigrant drumming with its public virtuosity, plus immediate continuity, for Latinos, with the live performance and communal participation of dance music throughout Latin America and the islands. Hippie counterculture from the

Photo by Jeremy Ayers

56

1960s forward, originating in enclaves like Santa Cruz and the Bay; hip-hop counterculture, from the mid-1970s forward, in the Bronx. Finally, amazingly, the increasing appearance of these cultures in leaderless, spontaneously coordinated, polyrhythmic and pluralist drum circles at the heart of new social movements—as a standard feature of them, along with the affinity groups and puppets, somehow manifesting forty years of alternative organization, from radical feminism and eco-anarchism, not just as entertainment, or spiritual practice, or a clarion sound (like twenty-first century hip-hop bagpipes), but an action and practice that *itself* seems to cross-pollinate with, and manifest, the new political and deliberative structures culminating in occupation—without words. With drums.

From this, the paradox: the drums drive talkers crazy! Insofar as the consensus model of assembly requires speech, speech, speech, but even more *listening*, in quiet and calm, to *hear* and take in another voice, in a way even parliamentary democracy (structured on antagonistic debate) does not; insofar as the drum circle, though also rooted in listening, depends on a kinetic, *continual*, unbroken, out-loud bodily manifestation of the rhythm, an experience of others' moves within a generality of constant movement, sound, and rhythm; and insofar as the essence of occupation is to exist in a common space where authority is not used to overrule anyone's form of life-giving expression—consensus and drumming seem put into jeopardy of mutual incomprehension. They're the same, somehow, and they make each other apeshit crazy.

And yet the scholarly literature does not seem to be up to date. References are incredibly sparse. One of the best, by far, is an introduction by the musicologist Eric Charry to the autobiography of the musician and cultural diplomat Babatunde Olatunji—a Nigerian grad student in public administration at NYU in the early 1950s who, out of funds and frustrated with American ignorance of African tradition and vile Southern racism (he took his BA at Morehouse), introduced Yoruba drumming to jazz circles. His bestselling album *Drums of*

Passion, from 1961, set the standard and expectations for "authentic" African drumming for the nation—even though it was actually recorded entirely with African-American and Afro-Caribbean drummers who lived in New York.

Cuban rhythms were central, and directly continuous with African inheritances, as was true for Brazil and Haiti. African-American music, however, was really a new creation of the polyglot nation. While John Coltrane, Max Roach, and others took up Olatunji for some of the great civil rights era masterpieces of American music, both Olatunji and others were building schools in Harlem and the Bronx to stimulate Black Pride (and Puerto Rican pride) and then Black Power, as African-American students reconnected to Africa. "The Congo Square drummers," Charry notes, "have been playing in what is called Drummer's Grove in Prospect Park, Brooklyn, since the late 1960s." (Congo Square was the famous field in New Orleans where African slaves and refugees of the Haitian and Santo Domingo revolts drummed and danced, one of—if not the only—such open sites in the nineteenth century.)

On the hippie West Coast in the late sixties, on beaches and in countercultural retreats like Esalen, hand drums were being taken up as a means of communal ecstasy and bonding. Arthur Hull, in Santa Cruz, published books and ran workshops to conceive of the drum circle for therapy, medical relief, and organization building. The hills and woods above UC Santa Cruz still house their share of drum circles on full moons, as do beaches from Marin County down to Venice in LA. Mickey Hart, second drummer for the Grateful Dead, expanded the length and range of percussion in the band's "Drums" interludes, which tens of thousands heard through tape culture, and parking-lot drum circle jams became a feature at Dead shows both among those who did and didn't have tickets to let them inside. When Mickey Hart brought Olatunji and his band to open for the Dead on New Year's Eve 1985 in Oakland, the two post-sixties traditions merged again. Olatunji toured with the Dead and, by the early 1990s, the Remo corporation started mass manufacturing a variety of environmentally-conscious, recycled-material African hand drums for the US market. Drum circles became a focus of communal gatherings like the Rainbow Gathering, held every year since 1972. Presumably, hand-drumming moved into activist circles through environmental channels first, traveling up and down the West Coast and crossing over with Latino culture. It never really returned to mesh with the African-American and East Coast protest cultures until, maybe, now.

In the anthropologist David Graeber's book documenting the protests at the Summit of the Americas in Quebec City in 2001, *Direct Action: An Ethnography*, the ethnographer-activist is briefly captivated by the mysterious appearance of drummers. "There was a sizeable band of drummers and other musicians a little bit up the slope, playing slow rhythmic music—actually, it was extremely good, with all sorts of intricate syncopation—and people dancing in hypnotic style. Occasionally someone would leave the human wall and join the dancing, or vice versa. Entranced, I fell away from the Bloc for a moment, promising I'd rendezvous later."

The only contemporary ethnography I've seen where an anthropologist did participant observation within a drum circle comes from a Turkish researcher, Hande Turgut Okan, who came from the Graduate Institute of Social Sciences in Istanbul to Venice Beach in 2007. The first thing that strikes you is who the "informants," when she interviews the circle, turn out to be:

My first informant was an African-American male. He was 71 years old. He was a retired Civil Engineer.... He was married and had four daughters.

My second informant was a 38-year-old white male. He was working as a machinist. ... He was single but had an 18-year-old daughter. He was living on a boat.

My third informant was 67 years old. He said his family had a blend of Polish, French, and German origins. He was a retired illustrator and a painter.... He used to design and create his musical instruments. His answer to my question about his inspiration of building his instruments was: 'I am inspired by poverty.'

My fourth informant was a 28-year-old African-American male. He was working as a paralegal . . . but he was also a musician.

My fifth informant was a 24-year-old male. His father was Moroccan and his mother was Spanish. He was still a student and wanted to transfer to UCLA to study Islamic Studies.

My sixth informant was originally German. He was 65 years old and had come to [the] USA 42 years ago.

In other words, in background, age, and racial or ethnic categorization, just about anybody participated, and not conforming to a class grouping. But also, conspicuously, all male—only one of the depth-interview sample of twelve was female. This was from a female anthropologist, who was not selecting for men. Zuccotti Park, similarly, has often seemed to have a preponderance of male drummers.

Turgut Okan's informants sound a bit like OWS participants when she asks about leaders, rules, and motivations for gathering with anonymous strangers to drum at the beach.

Everybody is doing what they wanna do, but I would say any one leader? No, everybody is a potential leader and depending on how much they wanna step up, anybody can start a song.

I don't think there are any [rules]. I think it's a self-regulatory unit. Everybody [has] to walk their own path and their own journey, make their own mistakes. So . . . I would say that it's more "free will regulatory."

If you would have to have a party and you had to invite 200 people to your private paradise island, I mean who would you invite? Would you invite some people from the Venice Beach Drum Circle or would you invite CEOs and people who would find their power in money?

Drumming is a part of my soul. That's how I look at it. It's part of my soul and it's a way of expressing myself creatively. I used to write poetry, but I haven't written poetry in a while.

Those of us on the outside of Zuccotti Park were pretty amazed, and sort of stupefied, when it looked as if, in the week or ten days leading up to October 25, a rift between drummers and the other constituencies of OWS were going to scuttle the New York occupation. The drum circles were stretching to performances that ran all day long and into the night. Local residents, represented by a community board, were sympathetic to the encampment but wanted enforcement of only two hours of daylight drumming per day. This seemed reasonable to the General Assembly but not to the drummers.

What made this so gruesome was partly that it seemed to reproduce a classic pairing within the dominant ideology. Domination loves to split mind and body, and this was being mapped onto assembly and circle: the drums became "ethnic," race-coded; the assembly, "white." The drums become male; the assembly, female. This didn't square with the racial and gendered realities of either group, but it grabbed hold of whatever quiddity it did seem to reflect. All of these polar divisions are things the occupation seeks to disenchant. They're pushed so deeply into our minds by power, though, that they are hard to root out. And whereas in the first two weeks of occupation the drummers were at the center of a shared space used by the assembly and everyone—playing by the stairs on Broadway, at the east—once the occupation grew, the drums moved, by agreement, to the west end of the park. The single group became two. This also meant the steadily growing community of drummers no longer had to stop for the nightly General Assembly. The GA began to notice that it was hard, on smaller-group nights, even to hear the human mic. Organizers talking in the park felt they couldn't hear themselves think. The circle of drummers started to feel that what they were doing wasn't ever recognized: couldn't anyone see that they were *doing* the movement, in effect; supporting it from the start, bringing in visitors and donations, but also *doing* it?

Yet the General Assembly got through this, too—largely, apparently, by talking, and listening, and listening, and talking, and refusing to act on a partial authority, at any key point, rather than getting the consensus of the whole. In a sense, the GA had already prepared themselves for being more like a drum circle, with the accidental innovation of the human mic. Hearers do respond to other people's particular cadences, in repeating them on their own bodies. It doesn't seem accidental that the invocation that gets it going and recovers its rhythms—"Mic check! *Mic check!*"—irresistibly frames all discussion with a phrasing adopted from hip hop, the great American art form of our time that still feels like a secret from the authorities. (Or that Russell Simmons, Kanye West, and Talib Kweli were among the first high-profile visitors and supporters.)

And the drum circle, for their part, formed a working group, thus ruling themselves into the peculiar way of talking (and meeting, and meeting some more) of the General Assembly and its developing spokes council structure. The choice of name for the working group was symbolically ingenious: PULSE, which not only speaks of the essential, though humble, guiding tempo around which a drum circle shifts and builds. PULSE also knits together the bodily metaphor, ending the mind/body split, in this measure of the vivacity of a person, something that races and slows with new thoughts and experiences, as well as with joy and fear.

SCENES FROM AN OCCUPA-TION

ASTRA TAYLOR

Sunday, October 9

Astra:

I went down to the park around noon to see friends and also to catch Slavoj Žižek speak. I wanted to see if the human microphone was up for the challenge, and it was. Žižek, of course, brought out the hits, but they were appropriately contextualized, and he was quite rousing in the end. Nothing like hearing everyone echoing him twice: "George Soros is a chocolate laxative." He also said some stuff people need to hear, like acknowledging, for example, the fact that leaderless movements usually still have leaders, they're just not out in the open. But he prefaced it by saying, "This may hurt some of your feelings, and I'm sorry," which was uncharacteristically sensitive of him.

Later I chatted with a fellow who has been part of OWS since the second planning meeting and was actually on the committee to find a spot to occupy. In the last few days there has been constant chatter about trying to start a second camp at Washington Square, but the problem, he explained, is that city parks close at midnight, which gives the police an excuse to boot out people who try to sleep in them. Bizarrely, Zuccotti Park can be held because it's private property and is officially open twenty-four hours a day. The park is a fluke of city zoning rules. Developers get to build higher than they would otherwise be allowed if they provide public open space in exchange. I read that Brookfield Properties, which owns Zuccotti, received $176 million in public subsidies. Whose park is it?

Today, I have to say, Zuccotti almost felt too full. Which is also why it's totally energizing and inspiring and, judging from this afternoon, the new tourist destination (though I think I saw somewhere this morning that Bloomberg said it was hurting tourism—definitely not true). If people overflow this plaza, what's the next step? I've heard that in Spain the big General Assembly dispersed/evolved into smaller neighborhood assemblies. Is it time for that here, or is it too soon?

ASTRA TAYLOR

Could we pull such a thing off or is it not the right move? I don't know, but it's interesting to think about.

Now that there are so many people involved in the protest, the General Assembly has become unwieldy. Some have proposed other methods of organization, like the spokes council model, which would introduce a bit of representation into the decision-making process by allowing each working group to empower a constantly rotating "spoke" who would communicate with the larger body. This model, proponents believe, would make things more efficient and accountable, increase working group autonomy, and better balance the rights and responsibilities of those involved with the movement. Why should a random person who shows up one night have as much say as someone who has been working in the kitchen, or volunteering with the legal team, or sleeping on the pavement for three weeks? Is that really fair? Others, however, remain steadfastly committed to the pure vision of direct democracy the GA represents. So far I like the GA model, but I worry it's more exclusionary than its advocates admit, since you have to be there in person to participate and you have to be quite assertive. More than that, a goodly portion of the 99 percent don't have the time to attend two long meetings a day, and I'm sure many wouldn't want to attend them if they did. Also, as Žižek presciently warned, as with every ostensibly leaderless movement, there seem to be things happening behind the scenes. From what I can tell, decisions are being made by various committees and working groups and by a wide variety of autonomous actors, not just through publicly deliberated group consensus. All things considered, I'm most sympathetic, and impressed, when I think of the general assemblies as a kind of political theater. On this level the GAs are absolutely brilliant, a vivid reminder of a kind of a democratic ideal our society seems to have totally abandoned.

DON'T FALL IN LOVE WITH YOURSELVES

SLAVOJ ŽIŽEK

Remarks at Zuccotti Park, October 9

We are all losers, but the true losers are down there on Wall Street. They were bailed out by billions of our money. We are called socialists, but here there is always socialism for the rich. They say we don't respect private property, but in the 2008 financial crash-down, more hard-earned private property was destroyed than if all of us here were to be destroying it night and day for weeks. They tell you we are dreamers. The true dreamers are those who think things can go on indefinitely the way they are. We are not dreamers. We are the awakening from a dream that is turning into a nightmare.

We are not destroying anything. We are only witnessing how the system is destroying itself. We all know the classic scene from cartoons. The cat reaches a precipice but it goes on walking, ignoring the fact that there is nothing beneath this ground. Only when it looks down and notices it, it falls down. This is what we are doing here. We are telling the guys there on Wall Street, "Hey, look down!"

In mid-April 2011, the Chinese government prohibited on TV, and in films and novels, all stories that contain alternate reality or time travel. This is a good sign for China. These people still dream about alternatives, so you have to prohibit this dreaming. Here we don't need a prohibition because the ruling system has even oppressed our capacity to dream. Look at the movies that we see all the time. It's easy to imagine the end of the world. An asteroid destroying all life and so on. But you cannot imagine the end of capitalism.

So what are we doing here? Let me tell you a wonderful old joke from Communist times. A guy was sent from East Germany to work in Siberia. He knew his mail would be read by censors, so he told his friends: "Let's establish a code. If a letter you get from me is written in blue ink, it is true what I say. If it is written in red ink, it is false." After a month, his friends get the first letter. Everything is in blue. It says, this letter: "Everything is wonderful here. Stores are full of good food. Movie theaters show good films from the West. Apartments are large and luxurious. The only thing you cannot buy is red ink." This is how we live. We have all the freedoms we want. But what we are missing is red ink: the language to articulate our non-freedom. The way we are taught to speak about freedom—war on terror and so on—falsifies freedom. And this is what you are doing here. You are giving all of us red ink.

There is a danger. Don't fall in love with yourselves. We have a nice time here. But remember, carnivals come cheap. What matters is the day after, when we will have to return to normal lives. Will there be any changes then? I don't want you to remember these days, you know, like, "Oh, we were young and it was beautiful." Remember that our basic message is, "We are allowed to think about alternatives." If the rule is broken, we do not live in the best possible world. But there is a long road ahead. There are truly difficult questions that confront us. We know what we do not want. But what do we want? What social organization can replace capitalism? What type of new leaders do we want?

SLAVOJ ŽIŽEK

Remember: the problem is not corruption or greed. The problem is the system. It forces you to be corrupt. Beware not only of the enemies, but also of false friends who are already working to dilute this process. In the same way you get coffee without caffeine, beer without alcohol, ice cream without fat, they will try to make this into a harmless moral protest. A decaffienated protest. But the reason we are here is that we have had enough of a world where to recycle Coke cans, to give a couple of dollars for charity, or to buy a Starbucks cappuccino where one percent goes to Third World starving children is enough to make us feel good. After outsourcing work and torture, after marriage agencies are now outsourcing our love life, we can see that for a long time, we allowed our political engagement also to be outsourced. We want it back.

We are not communists if communism means a system which collapsed in 1990. Remember that today those communists are the most efficient, ruthless capitalists. In China today, we have capitalism which is even more dynamic than your American capitalism, but it doesn't need democracy. Which means when you criticize capitalism, don't allow yourself to be blackmailed that you are against democracy. The marriage between democracy and capitalism is over. The change is possible.

What do we perceive today as possible? Just follow the media. On the one hand, in technology and sexuality, everything seems to be possible. You can travel to the moon, you can become immortal by biogenetics, you can have sex with animals or whatever, but look at the field of society and economy. There, almost everything is considered impossible. You want to raise taxes by a little bit for the rich. They tell you it's impossible—we lose competitivity. You want more money for health care, they tell you, "Impossible, this means totalitarian state." There's something wrong in the world where you are promised to be immortal but cannot spend a little bit more for healthcare. Maybe we need to set our priorities straight here. We don't want a higher standard of living. We want a better standard of living. The only sense in which we are communists is that we care for the commons. The commons of nature. The commons of knowledge, privatized by intellectual property. The commons of biogenetics. For this, and only for this, we should fight.

Communism failed absolutely, but the problems of the commons are here. They are telling you we are not American here. But the conservative fundamentalists who claim they really are American have to be reminded of something: What is Christianity? It's the holy spirit. What is the holy spirit? It's an egalitarian community of believers who are linked by love for each other, and who only have their own freedom and responsibility to do it. In this sense, the holy spirit is here now. And down there on Wall Street, there are pagans who are worshipping blasphemous idols. So all we need is patience. The only thing I'm afraid of is that we will someday just go home and then we will meet once a year, drinking beer and nostaligically remembering "what a nice time we had here." Promise yourselves that this will not be the case. We know that people often desire something but do not really want it. Don't be afraid to really want what you desire.

"THE TIMES THEY ARE AH- " CHANGIN'....

THE SONGS THEY ARE THE SA-A ME.

David Kearns, "Occupation Sketchbook"

SCENES FROM AN OCCUPA- TION

ASTRA TAYLOR & SARAH RESNICK

Monday, October 10

Astra:

I actually made it to OWS for a bit today. Can't stay away. The first thing I noticed was a man with a large sign, "Google: Zionists Control Wall Street," and I cringed, briefly worried that creeps had taken over the occupation. A few minutes later I found myself talking to someone who has been camping there for the last few weeks and he mentioned, out of the blue, that he thought the guy was an agent provocateur because his poster was getting more and more inflammatory with each passing day. About an hour later I was relieved to see two middle-aged women chasing the man around the park, flanking him and holding signs that read "Who pays this guy? He doesn't speak for me or OWS!" I cheered them on, as did others.

The best thing, though, was when a small group of folks recognized my husband, Jeff Mangum, since we showed up a few nights ago and he sang some songs to those who wanted to listen. "Hey," a girl yelled as we were strolling through the park, "will you join sanitation?" So he spent a good amount of time in gloves sorting recycling. The entertainers should clean too. Now that's revolutionary.

Sarah R:

"This march needs more balls!" yelled a tall, twenty-something man in plaid shirt and jeans, his face painted in zombie likeness. It was a Monday night, well past 9 PM, and about forty of us were marching up Broadway, wielding slogan-filled placards and cycling through the usual catalog of chants. A woman in her early twenties held a small snare drum behind her back while her friend followed behind her, banging out the beat. The group was ragtag, though mostly young, and displayed much of the now-familiar iconography adopted by demonstrators of the past several years: Guy Fawkes masks (made famous by the film *V for Vendetta*), the zombie makeup, Anonymous flags and t-shirts. There was at least one anarcho-hassid—a subculture until then unknown to me—waving a small red-and-black flag.

The grievance was seemingly directed at the absence of incident. True: Were one to compare it to the clashes with riot police, or the 700 arrests on the Brooklyn Bridge, it was an uneventful march. Nothing much happened. The group had formed out of the Liberty Plaza encampment, heeding a fellow protester's call to march. When they passed us heading south on Church Street, my friend James and I tagged along; we were bewildered yet somewhat thrilled by the initial absence of police accompaniment—a rarity in New York City demonstrations. The police would, of course, join us in due time, but for a brief period we were unchaperoned, free to take the street. James, electing himself provocateur, overturned a wooden police barrier then banged on the gate of a nearby storefront. "This. Is. A peace-ful pro-test," the group retorted. And with that we returned to the plaza to recruit more marchers.

From there we pushed onward, snaking through the narrow roadways of the Financial District as residents gaped from their four- and five-story vantages, the dimly-lit rectangles of their camera phones visible from below. The police were alongside us now; we were back on the sidewalk. We made conversation with the strangers among us. A man in a navy pinstripe suit towed behind and asked when we planned to stop ruining the lives of the children; they hadn't slept in three weeks. "I'm on your side," he told me. "I used to live in a mansion. I lost everything and now I live in a two bedroom apartment. But the children need to sleep." We had no plan, no stated objective, but to walk—to be visible, audible, that was all. There were no confrontations, no batons unsheathed, no whistles, no shouting, no force of any kind. The cops looked bored, worn, distracted even—the protest had its longueurs.

NYPD AND OWS: A CLASH OF STYLES

ALEX VITALE

Occupy Wall Street's defiant style of nonviolent protest has consistently clashed with the NYPD's obsession with order maintenance policing, resulting in hundreds of mostly unnecessary arrests and a significant infringement on the basic rights of free speech and assembly. The origins of this conflict can be found in the rise of public disorder in the 1980s and NYPD's embrace of order maintenance policing in the 1990s.

The 1980s witnessed an explosion in public disorder on New York's streets. The city was still reeling from the massive collapse of its budget in the mid-1970s, while continuing deindustrialization meant a scarcity of jobs for the working class. Growth in other sectors—homelessness, prostitution, graffiti, and street-level drug dealing—followed accordingly. This explosion of public disorder coincided handily with a change in the city's class composition. Having watched the city's tax base disappear, Mayor Ed Koch would spend most of his two terms cravenly (and successfully) soliciting the return of corporate headquarters. The result was the total reorientation of the city toward real estate, insurance, and finance, whose crisply white-collared employees were decidedly unenthusiastic about New York's "grittiness" and began to demand that the NYPD be more responsive to "quality of life" concerns. This posed a challenge to the NYPD's longstanding professional crime-fighter ethos, which had prioritized making felony arrests that led to convictions. In their position as the front end of the criminal justice system, the NYPD emphasized strict adherence to the legal necessities of the court system; alleviating the seemingly more mundane nuisance issues raised by residents was something many police viewed as beyond or even beneath their area of expertise.

By the early 1990s, however, a new paradigm of policing, based on the "broken windows" theory of crime, would demand that police become social activists of a certain kind, whether they liked it or not. The "broken windows" theory, first aired in the *Atlantic Monthly* by social scientists James Q. Wilson and George L. Kelling and widely discussed thereafter, held that one could fight serious crime and restore communities by controlling low-level disorder. "Broken windows"–based policing emphasizes the aggressive "zero tolerance" control of minor disorderly activity such as drinking in public, aggressive panhandling, graffiti, street prostitution, and drug dealing. This new approach, associated with Mayor Giuliani, was actually already well underway during the Dinkins administration. But it was Police Commissioner William Bratton who institutionalized it throughout the NYPD. Previously ignored problems like turnstile jumping, public intoxication, squeegee men, and aggressive panhandling were moved to the top of the enforcement agenda. Extensive research has called into question the basic linkage between disorder and serious crime and highlighted the essentially conservative nature of this theory, which calls on more aggressive policing to restore communities as an alternative to additional city services, new investment, or improved economic opportunities for the poor. But "broken windows" may have succeeded less on evidence of its effectiveness and more on its power as a moralistic theory of crime-fighting; it signified a moral imperative to restore middle class values to the city's public spaces, which broadly accorded with the city's new urban elites.

One of the most emblematic, pervasive, and pernicious forms of this new style of policing is the ubiquitous use of "stop and frisk" tactics in communities of color. Hundreds of thousands of New Yorkers are routinely stopped each year with little legal basis in hopes of preempting criminal behavior through an aggressive intrusion into people's private activities. The NYPD strongly believes that this kind of aggressive proactive order maintenance policing is responsible for the city's remarkable crime drop over the last twenty years, though similar drops across the country belie the distinctive contribution of "broken windows"–based policing.

Increasingly, black and Latino community leaders and progressive politicians have also begun bravely to reject the intellectual and moral prestige of "broken windows," labeling it as either a form of racial profiling or a violation of the basic constitutional right to be free from unreasonable police

ALEX VITALE

searches. Combined with growing challenges to the heavy-handed and at times unlawful enforcement of marijuana laws, serious questions have been raised about the appropriateness of this intrusive style of policing. In the past year, several new coalitions have emerged to challenge this form of policing, and direct actions targeting local police precincts have occurred in Harlem and Central Brooklyn in recent weeks.

+ + +

However, there continues to be a less well-known adaptation of order maintenance policing—the policing of demonstrations. In 1991, then First Deputy Commissioner Ray Kelly devised a system for controlling the Crown Heights riots through the aggressive use of arrest teams. The area of disturbance was divided up into zones, and the arrest team for each zone was instructed to make as many arrests as possible for any type of legal violation in an attempt to proactively and preemptively set a tone of police control on the streets.

Later, in 1996, there was a large public celebration of a Yankee World Series victory at City Hall Park. Then Manhattan South Bureau Chief Allan Hoehl, concerned that there might be a crushing incident in the park, devised a system of controlling access through choke points, subdividing the crowd, and creating intermittent "frozen zones" to allow access to the area by police and EMS.

Of course, these weren't demonstrations, but the forms of policing developed to deal with them were translated for protest marches and rallies nonetheless—a fatal elision that would have consequences for protests up to the present day. In addition to the use of barriers and arrest teams, this system limits the issuing of permits for marches and rallies and uses force against people for minor violations of the law in an attempt to preempt further trouble down the road. In most cases this merely hinders protests, leaving them disempowered and isolated from the public. In a few cases, though, these restrictions have led to serious escalations of conflict as police tried to micromanage large crowds.

The most dramatic example of this was in 2003, when the NYPD denied a march permit to United for Peace and Justice on the eve of the US invasion of Iraq. Instead, UFPJ was forced to hold a stationary rally that attracted at least a quarter of a million people. The police deployed tens of thousands of steel barriers and thousands of police officers to tightly regulate a peaceful, permitted demonstration. The result of this attempt at over-control was that hundreds of thousands of people spilled into the streets, unable to access the demonstration area because of the overuse of choke points and "frozen zones." In the end, police attacked these demonstrators with mounted units and pepper spray. Hundreds were arrested, dozens injured, and hundreds of thousands of people had their basic right to protest denied to them.

Similar problems emerged in 2004, during the Republican National Convention. Permits were denied for Central Park and other traditional protest locations, barricades were used extensively at permitted demonstrations, and over a thousand people were preemptively arrested, with all the charges being quickly dropped by the Manhattan DA.

This pattern remains in place in the police handling of the Occupy Wall Street demonstrations. While many of these demonstrations have been disruptive, they have been overwhelmingly nonviolent in character. The police response, however, has been to focus intensively on each minor legal violation and respond with heavy-handed enforcement actions, which in some cases exceed their legal authority and violate protestors' basic rights to free speech and assembly.

Consider what has precipitated the vast majority of the arrests in this movement: using a megaphone, writing on the sidewalk with chalk, marching in the street (and Brooklyn Bridge), standing in line at a bank to close an account, and occupying a public park past closing. These are all nonviolent, if disruptive, forms of political expression. To the police, however, they are all disorderly conduct, and in keeping with the "broken windows" theory, they require swift and harsh police enforcement actions.

Unfortunately for the police, it is exactly this disorderliness that has energized this movement. For years, think tanks, labor unions, and progressive politicians have railed against the corrupt marriage between financial and political elites to no avail. Millions of Facebook posts, tweets, and policy white papers have failed to galvanize a mass movement. Instead, it was the occupation of public spaces, marching without permits, and disruption of daily life in the Financial District that signaled an open-ended defiance lacking in previous efforts.

As a result of this clash of styles, demonstrators continue to resist the tight controls of the NYPD by refusing to move

Drawing by Celeste Dupuy-Spencer

onto the sidewalk or by attempting to go over or around barriers, and the police have responded with high levels of force.
And this use of force has not been the uncontrolled acts of
rank-and-file officers lacking supervision or training. The violence has almost entirely come from high-ranking command
staff, so-called "white shirts," who are lieutenants or higher.
The use of these supervising officers in the front lines may
have been an attempt to reduce police violence, with the assumption that more experienced officers would show better
judgment. Instead, their subsequent behaviour suggests that
a culture of control, violence, and impunity pervades the entire department.

It was Deputy Inspector Anthony Bologna, who has decades
of experience as both a precinct commander and in managing
demonstrations, who pepper-sprayed several young women
peacefully standing behind orange netting on the sidewalk
on September 24. In fact, he is a defendant in some of the liti-
gation stemming from illegal preemptive arrests during the
2004 RNC and recently received a loss of ten vacation days for
the pepper-spraying incident. Another high-ranking officer
was recorded wildly swinging his baton at demonstrators and
reporters during a standoff at Wall Street and Broadway on
October 5. More recently, Deputy Inspector Johnny Cardona
was caught on camera on October 14, grabbing a young man
from behind, twisting him around, and punching him in the
face, causing serious injury.

The NYPD is facing a major challenge. Their attempts at
using mass arrests on the Brooklyn Bridge on October 1 to in-
timidate the demonstrators was unsuccessful; their efforts to
corral them into protest pens and keep them on the sidewalks
has not worked either; and police violence has only helped
fuel the movement and brought disrepute and political trouble for the NYPD. A long tense standoff may be in the offing
with frequent arrests and occasional outbursts of police violence as demonstrators' defiance comes up against police
intolerance.

Since the mayor's failed attempt to clear out Liberty Plaza on October 14, the police seem to have taken a step back from their zero-tolerance approach. People are now able to use tents and tarps in the park, and no one is being arrested for the heinous crime of writing with chalk on the sidewalk, though arrests continue to occur at sit-ins and street marches. This scaling back of aggressive policing represents a significant expansion of First Amendment rights that have been severely eroded over the last forty years by a broad array of "time, place, and manner" restrictions that Occupy Wall Street demonstrators have rejected.

While the policing of OWS in New York has become more accommodating, officials in many other cites have carried out dramatic and sometimes violent evictions of occupation demonstrators. In many cases, however, this has served to build these local efforts and keep the media spotlight on this growing movement. The level of activity nationally and internationally also suggests that whatever the fate of individual encampments are over the coming winter, there will be a resurgence of contentious, disorderly, and defiant protest across the country in the spring.

NYPD AND OWS

David Kearns, "Occupation Sketchbook"

SCENES FROM AN OCCUPA- TION

SARAH LEONARD & KEITH GESSEN

Thursday, October 13

Sarah L:

On Thursday night, the occupation was threatened by a Bloombergian assault by sanitation crew—Liberty Plaza must be powerwashed! It was all full of hippies, and the park's corporate owners issued a bizarre letter asking for police aid in washing it down to prevent a "public health risk." The occupiers responded by scrubbing the living hell out of the park, top to bottom, east to west, so that all night the plaza smelled like vinegar. The call went out for supporters to show up in the early morning en masse to defend the park.

And so we did, legal aid number scrawled on skin, no valuables, hundreds and hundreds of people ready to risk arrest for the birthplace of a movement sweeping the country. And as everyone was warned of the risks via the people's mic, word came from corporate headquarters: the cleaning had been postponed. A cheer went up. Our bodies had been enough this time, and we decamped to occupy breakfast and watch a disappointed NY1 reporter on television, trying to salvage a story from this gloriously solidaristic non-arrest.

Keith:

I liked how the human mic broke down during the announcement. It was working really well as the speaker explained that anyone who stayed in the park could get arrested, and those who didn't want to get arrested should cross to the other side of the street and bear witness from there. The park was packed, we were way in the back, but four waves of the human mic allowed each word to reach us. Then a young woman came forward with an announcement. It sounded like this:

I'd like to read a brief statement
from Deputy Mayor Holloway:
We received notice from the owners of Zuccotti Park
[Wild cheering]

Friday, October 14

Sarah L:

Friday night was all about the packed discussion at Bluestockings, hosted by the young magazine *Jacobin*, unofficially a contentious faceoff between anarchists and socialists about the direction of the emerging movement. The moderator, *Jacobin* editor-at-large Seth Ackerman, valiantly held a sort of peace between panelists who rapidly shifted in demeanor from comrades to antagonists. The anarchists, *New York Times* freelance reporter Natasha Lennard and writer/editor Malcolm Harris of *The New Inquiry* and *Jacobin*, talked about the liberated subjectivities emerging in the chaotic now. The other side of the table—economics journalist Doug Henwood, Chris Maisano, editor of Democratic-Socialist paper *The Activist*, and political theorist Jodi Dean—argued variations on the need for greater organization, for achievable political goals based in communalism, and for some sort of engagement with the state.

The debate was lively, rife with condescension in both directions, and did feel, comfortingly, like a throwback to a time when politics mattered. When Lennard argued that the power with which the protesters should concern themselves was not that of the state or of finance, but the Foucauldian power that "coded" us all and inscribed neoliberalism into our very being, Henwood retorted that he suspected people wanted jobs, "not to re-code their heads." When Maisano suggested recruiting students to the cause at local colleges, Lennard leaned forward eagerly. "Recruitment? Don't you think that's a bit fascistic?" A little part of me died right there, and I thought Henwood was going to choke.

Regardless, the anarchists perhaps find greatest joy in the movement, and people who actually know how to organize will be critical to its future. An essay by Michael Walzer came to mind, where he argues that our utopia on the left resides in the movement itself. Something about the debate's focus on different sets of ideals and the real inability to talk about concrete next steps felt like it was forgetting that joy and construction are often two sides of the same coin. As Walzer says about the eternal fight for social democracy, "The goodness is in the work as much as in the benefits—so it doesn't matter if the work goes on and on, as it does. It is important and worthwhile work because of its mutuality, because of the talents and capacities it calls forth, and because of the moral value it embodies. That work is socialism-in-the-making, and that is the only socialism we will ever know."

SARAH LEONARD & KEITH GESSEN

Sunaura Taylor, "Corporate Welfare"

CLAIMING DIVISION, NAMING A WRONG

JODI DEAN

Occupy Wall Street rejects the fantasy that "what's good for Wall Street is good for Main Street" to claim the division between Wall Street and Main Street and name this division a fundamental wrong, the wrong of inequality, exploitation, and theft. "We are the 99%" highlights the gap between the wealth of the top one percent and the rest of us. It politicizes a statistic that expresses capitalism's reliance on fundamental inequality—"we" can never all be counted as the top one percent. In so doing, the slogan asserts a collectivity. It does not unify this collectivity under a substantial identity—race, ethnicity, religion, nationality. Rather it asserts it as the "we" of a divided people, the people divided between expropriators and expropriated. In the setting of an occupied Wall Street, this "we" is a class, one of two opposed and hostile classes, those who have and control wealth, and those who do not.

"We are the 99%" also erases the multiplicity of individuated, partial, and divided interests that fragment and weaken the people as the rest of us. Against capital's constant attempts to pulverize and decompose the collective people, the claim of the 99% responds with the force of a belonging that not only cannot be erased but that capital's own methods of accounting produce. Capital has to measure itself, count its profits, its rate of profit, its share of profit, its capacity to leverage its profit, its confidence or anxiety in its capacity for future profit. Capital counts and analyzes who has what, representing to itself the measures of its success. In the slogan "We are the 99%" these numbers are put to use, claimed as the subjectivation of the gap separating the top one percent from the rest of us. With this claim, the gap becomes a vehicle for the expression of communist desire, for a politics that asserts the people as a divisive force in the interest of over-turning present society and making a new one anchored in collectivity and the common.

Three moves prominent in discussions of OWS attempt to fill in or occlude the gap the movement installs: democratization, moralization, and individualization.

"Democratization" designates efforts to frame the movement in terms of American electoral politics. One of the most

JODI DEAN

common tendencies is to treat OWS as the Tea Party of the left. So construed, the movement isn't something radically new; it's derivative. The Tea Party has already been there and done that. This analogy fails to acknowledge that the Tea Party is astro-turf, organized by Dick Armey and funded by the Koch brothers. A further democratizing move reduces the movement to the 2012 elections: what does Occupy Wall Street mean for Obama? Does it strengthen the Democratic Party? Will it pull it back toward the center? This democratizing move omits the obvious question: if it were about Obama and the Democratic Party, it would be about Obama and the Democratic Party—not marches, strikes, occupations, and arrests.

A related democratization advises the movement to pursue any number of legislative paths, seek constitutional amendments to deny corporations personhood, change campaign finance laws, and abolish the Federal Reserve Bank. The oddness of these suggestions, the way they attempt to make the movement something it is not, appears as soon as one recalls what the protesters are doing: occupying. In New York, they are sleeping outside in a privately-owned park, attempting to reach consensus on a wide range of issues affecting their daily life together (what sort of coffee to serve, how to keep the park clean, how to keep people warm and dry, what to do about the drummers, how to spend the money that comes in to support the movement, what the best ways to organize discussions are, and so on). Democratization skips the actual fact of occupation, reframing the movement in terms of a functional political system. If the system were functional, people wouldn't be occupying all over the country—not to mention the world: an additional effect of the democratic reduction is reformatting a global movement against capitalism into US-specific concerns with our dysfunctional electoral system.

Finally, an additional democratization begins from the assumption that the movement is essentially a democratic one, that its tactics and concerns are focused on the democratic process. It then criticizes occupation for being a non-democratic

tactic. Protesters are rejecting democratic institutions, breaking the law, disrupting public space, squandering public
resources (police overtime can get expensive) and attempting
to assert the will of a minority of vocal protesters outside of
and in contradiction to democratic procedures. This criticism
exposes the incoherence in the democratization argument
overall: occupation is not a democratic strategy; it is a mili-
tant, divisive tactic that expresses the fundamental division
on which capitalism depends.

The second mode of division's erasure is moralization,
treating OWS in exclusively moral terms. The true contribution of the movement is said to be its transformation of the
common sense of what is just and what is unjust. This line of
commentary emphasizes greed and corruption, commending
the movement for opening our eyes to the need to get things
in order, to clean house. Moralization occludes division as
it remains stuck in a depoliticizing liberal formula of ethics
and economics. Rather than acknowledging the failure of the
capitalist system, the contemporary collapse of its neoliberal
form, and the contradictions that are demolishing capitalism from within (global debt crises, unsustainable patterns
of consumption, climate change, the impossibility of continued accumulation at the rate necessary for capitalist growth,
mass unemployment and unrest), moralization proceeds as if
a couple of bad apples—a Bernie Madoff here, a rogue trader
there—let their greed get out of control. It then extends this
idea of corruption (rather than systemic failure), blaming the
"culture of Wall Street" or even the consumerism of the entire country, as if the US were a whole and as a whole needed
spiritual cleansing and renewal. Moralization treats OWS as a
populist movement, mediating it in populist terms of a whole
people engaging in the ritual of repentance, renewal, and reform. It proceeds as if the division OWS claims were a kind of
infection to be cured rather than a fundamental antagonism
that has been disavowed.

The third attempt to eliminate the gap comes from individualization. Here an emphasis on individual choice displaces

JODI DEAN

the movement's collectivity. On the one hand, OWS is treated as a smorgasbord of issues. Occupiers and supporters are just non-partisan individuals cherry-picking their concerns and exercising their rights of free speech and assembly. On the other hand are the movement's basic practices: decisions must be reached by consensus, no one can speak for another, each person has to be affirmed as autonomously supporting whatever the GA undertakes. In each case, individualism not only supercedes collectivity, but it also effaces the rupture between the occupation and US culture more generally, a culture that celebrates and cultivates individuality and personalization. Given that the strength of OWS draws from collectivity, an experience amplified by the people's mic, to emphasize individuality is to misunderstand the common at the heart of the movement. It reinserts the movement within the dominant culture, as if occupation were a choice like any other, as if choices weren't themselves fantasies that individuals actually could determine their own lives or make a political difference in the context of the capitalist system and the class power of the top one percent.

Democratization, moralization, and individualization attempt to restore a fantastic wholeness where OWS asserts a fundamental division. Whether as a democratic political system, a moral community, or the multiplicity of individuals, this fantasy is one that denies the antagonism on which capitalism relies: between those who have to sell their labor power to survive and those who do not, between those who not only have no choice but to sell their labor power but nonetheless cannot and those who command, steer, and gamble upon the resources and futures of the rest of us for their own enjoyment.

The three modes of disavowing division miss the power of occupation as a tactic that asserts a gap by forcing a presence. This forcing is more than simply of people into places where they do not belong (even when they may ostensibly have a right). It's a forcing of collectivity over individualism, the combined power of a group that disrupts a space readily accommodating of individuals. Such a forcing puts in stark relief the conceit of a political arrangement that claims to represent a people who cannot be present, a divided people who, when present, instill such fear and insecurity that they have to be met by armed police and miles of barricades. It asserts the class division prior to and unremedied by democracy under capitalism.

That Occupy Wall Street brings to the fore the fundamental antagonism of class conflict is born out even in the slogan "Occupy Everything." The slogan seems at first absurd: we already occupy everything, so how can we occupy everything? What matters is the minimal difference, the shift in perspective that the injunction to occupy effects. We have to occupy in a different mode, assert our being there in and for itself, for the common, not for the few, the one percent. The shift in perspective created by "Occupy Everything" intensifies the gap between what has been and what can be, what "capitalist realism" told us was the only alternative and what the actuality of the movement forced us to wake up to. The gap it names is the gap of communist desire, a collective desire for collectivity: we occupy everything because it is already ours in common.

JODI DEAN

Joanna Neborsky

SCENES FROM AN OCCUPA- TION

SARAH RESNICK, SARAH LEONARD & ASTRA TAYLOR

Saturday, October 15

Sarah R:

At 5 PM, I was part of a group of fifty or so that made its way from the steps of the New York Public Library to the massive convergence at Times Square. We were united under a banner—the writers and artists affinity group. We were friends, colleagues, acquaintances, and there was a palpable sense of anticipation; this evening there would be other occupation attempts, we were told. The movement would expand. We marched up Avenue of the Americas eager to join the demonstration, many of us with the same poster: "Money talks—too much. Occupy!"

After several route diversions and a subsequent, though temporary, confusion, we eventually settled into the crowd near the junction of Broadway and Seventh Avenue. The sun had started to set, though it seemed no darker in the enduring glow of the animated LED advertisements. A lingerie-clad model, terrifying at ten stories tall . . . We cheered and ardently held our signs above us, a shield of sorts. (Though the area's porn theaters and peep shows have now long disappeared, a more sinister perversion persists.) Soon after, the question emerged: Now what? Was anything else happening? Was there no other plan?

Anxiety briefly settled on those of us more prone to claustrophobic tendencies—we were in the midst of thousands, cordoned in by police who had begun to exercise tactics of intimidation with horses and riot gear. Intermittent waves of muted agitation were offset by amiable chatter with strangers and friends alike (usually OWS related), a sighting of the hipster cop, and a rendition of Harry Dixon Loes's "This Little Light of Mine," sung by hundreds (thousands?) in unison. And because apparently no act of protest is complete without a drum circle, one soon emerged (much to the discomfort of all others in the tightly-packed vicinity).

Every so often, a raving and indignant middle-aged man pushed through our group. "Next time," he bawled, "don't obey the police!" We were berated for our apparent rout: our refrain from shoving through the barricades, our cowardice at confronting the police lines, our unmistakable failure to act. Nettled by his accusation, I thought back to Monday's impromptu march and the grumbling of the zombie protester: "This march needs more balls." Did we? (Of course, more than thirty people were arrested but one street over.) What stood to be gained from our mere standing in place, en masse?

Later that evening, other criticisms of the Times Square convergence emerged, albeit from more reasoned voices: the act was disorganized, disjointed, there was no identifiable plan, no strategy—we had effectively done nothing. Instead, we should be directing our resources toward considered action. I nodded sympathetically; I agreed. I still do. Though I noted a commonality among these various criticisms: an anxiety toward idleness. And it struck me that this idleness could potentially be redeemed. Acts of protest wouldn't—needn't—always meet a preordained objective or outcome, a prompt reaction or result, cause and effect. We were taking up space, filling up time—and inaction, boredom, even listlessness would sometimes play a part, and they too have value. For these acts resonate in the realm of the symbolic, but they operate in the social too. Ideas are exchanged. New friendships emerge, old ones solidify. Restlessness foments action.

Sarah L:

Later Saturday night, everyone reconvened in Washington Square Park for a big General Assembly, calm and well-organized, run through the people's mic and a "progressive stack." Cops at the park entrances warned arrivees of its midnight closing time.

Debate raged over whether protesters could hold the park and whether it was a good target. One NYU student suggested that if everyone took the park, NYU students would emerge from the surrounding buildings to help. Eyebrows shot upward. Consensus seemed to be emerging that the park was too big to hold, so I took a little wander around as the midnight hour of confrontation drew nigh.

There were little contingents of blue-jacketed NYPD Community Affairs people all over, and white shirts made periodic announcements reminding the assembled protesters of the curfew. But the spectacle of force was under the white triumphal arch on the north side of the park. Several rows of helmeted police stood in formation, ready to march into the park at the stroke of midnight. It was tiring to see all this again, probably tiring for everyone, and most protesters headed peacefully out of the park, many marching back to Liberty Plaza to maintain the occupied space. "Let us raise a standard to which the wise and the honest can repair," reads the arch. "The event is in the hand of God." Thus spake George Washington to the Constitutional Convention, another discursive assembly of sorts, albeit with a considerably less progressive stack and no anarchists. It was a pleasure to see protesters disperse, not swept before a wave of pepper spray, but for tactical reasons, after reaching a thoughtful and reasoned democratic consensus, or as near one as possible, and trucking back to home base to fight another day.

Sunday, October 16

Astra:

This afternoon I heard there were plans brewing for a second occupation. The site: the BMW Guggenheim Lab, a temporary corporate-sponsored space housed in a large community garden on Houston Street near Second Avenue.

I first heard about the idea four days prior, when I got the following email from a friend:

> *hey y'all*
> *so I got word that last night at the ows art & culture meeting an announcement was made that the committee was invited to present at BMW Lab . . . seems like that Lab might need some sleeping bags . . . it is slated to CLOSE for good on OCTOBER 16 (four days from today) so maybe that can be*

*turned into occupier housing and neighborhood assembly
meeting spot*

Though farther from Wall Street, the location was ideal in
many ways. The Lab was equipped with a kitchen, eating area,
covered shelter, and several bathrooms. The garden itself was
spacious and highly visible.

Would-be occupiers made plans to show up during the
closing party, which was supposed to end at 10:30 PM. The
General Assembly, they promised, would start at 10:31. When
I arrived a little after 9 PM, however, the celebration was already shut down, the plot foiled. The DJ was packing up, the
garbage bags were being filled, security had emptied everyone
out, and a cop car was parked outside with the lights flashing.
About thirty people still milled around on the sidewalk, some
with camping gear tucked under their arms. They seemed in
good spirits, though they'd have to sleep elsewhere.

I, for one, was a bit disappointed there wasn't more of a
showdown, if only to call attention to the situation's irony.
As my friend's email made clear, the team behind BMW
Guggenheim Lab had been eager to glom onto OWS. For example, only a few days ago the Lab had offered a Wall Street
Occupation Tour. "Public spaces have been contested
throughout the history of New York," the calendar page explained. "Now hundreds of activists are camped out in the
heart of the Financial District. What are the written and un-
written rules that govern how we use public spaces? How have
they changed over time? What happens when activists contest
those rules? Join us on a tour from the BMW Guggenheim Lab
to the Financial District, where we will interview occupation
participants and consider the past, present, and future of the
commons." On another website an article published with the
Lab's imprimatur analyzed the Zuccotti Park encampment as
an "ecosystem," lavishing praise on the ingenious compost
and trash systems, the well-stocked library, and the spirit of
volunteerism. "Rather than a protest," the article enthused,

"Occupy Wall Street is an inspirational model for an alternative future."

Inspirational from a distance, of course. When the Occupy ecosystem reached their doorstep, BMW Guggenheim called the police. They would not let the party become a protest. And so the demonstrators drifted off into the night. I hope they come back and try again, if not at this park, then elsewhere, everywhere.

Dan Archer, "Occupied Oakland"

CHINA-TOWN IS NOWHERE

AUDREA LIM

I remember the day I first felt Chinatown's absence from Zuccotti Park. I was listening to people giving interviews on-site, but embarrassingly, all I could think about was food. The kitchen had just run out.

Evictions! Foreclosures! Medical bills! Student loans! Jobs!

People were talking about how these things had brought them to the park. I was contemplating the prospect of my fifth falafel that week, having ruled out a ten-dollar sandwich, when it hit me—Chinatown! The land of impossibly cheap food. It took just a couple of minutes by bike. Chinatown is less than a mile away from Zuccotti Park.

A couple of things occurred to me as I ate. The first was that visitors to Zuccotti should regularly stop by Chinatown and buy loads of food—dollar dumplings, dollar noodles, dollar treats of all sorts—to donate to the kitchen. They could help keep the occupation alive using little more than loose change, while also supporting the immigrant, working-class Chinatown vendors. A no-brainer.

The other thing was that Chinatown is the last poor immigrant community in lower Manhattan (alongside the Lower East Side, with which it overlaps), yet it has nearly no presence in OWS. Nor is Chinatown ever raised in conversations about Wall Street versus the 99 percent, even though evictions, low-wage jobs, lack of social services, and tenant abuse have been daily occurrences for Chinatown's residents since long before the 2008 financial crisis—or the one before that, or even the one before that. In fact, Chinatown, now over a century old, has never stopped being economically, politically, and culturally marginalized, but despite its proximity to Zuccotti Park, OWS hasn't noticed it at all.

Let me give a very brief overview of how Chinatown has always been "part of the 99 percent."

In the nineteenth century, the first Chinese laborers were brought to the US under slave-like conditions to work the California gold mines, filling the cheap labor vacuum left by the emancipation of black slaves. When the 1870s depression hit, the rise of the Workingman's Party, the great champion of California's 99 percent, proclaimed that "The Chinese Must Go!" (complaints repeated nearly verbatim in immigration debates today), and the Chinese Exclusion Act was passed in 1882. Chinese immigration was put to a halt, and racial discrimination against the Chinese became further institutionalized. Beatings and lynchings were the norm, including the 1885 Rock Springs, Wyoming, massacre of twenty-eight Chinese miners. In search of less hostile atmospheres, Chinese immigrants dispersed eastward and concentrated in major cities with preexisting pockets of Chinese. This included New York City.

Facing discrimination in the labor market, and barred from public employment and many professional trades (barbers, plumbers, and chauffeurs) due to lack of citizenship, many Chinese took up low-wage service jobs that continue to be known as "Chinese" professions—laundrymen and restaurant workers, for instance. Less desirable to other Americans, these jobs also required little personal capital, few English-language skills, and minimal contact with the outside world. Excluded from society, Chinese immigrants also formed their own systems of political organization and mutual economic and social support.

In the mid-twentieth century, the garment factories moved to Chinatown. The growth of public and welfare services in the US made low-paying, grueling sweatshop work less attractive to most American citizens, at the same time as a steady stream of Chinese laborers was flowing into the US. Seeing opportunity, much of New York's garment industry relocated from Midtown. The number of Chinatown women working in sweatshops—for twelve to fifteen hours, seven days a week, under dismal conditions and for minimal pay—grew from 8,000 in 1969 to 20,000 in 1982. Meanwhile, the population of Chinatown swelled, and the neighborhood's densely concentrated sub-standard tenement buildings, long neglected by building-code inspectors, grew more overcrowded still.

In the 1970s, both the civil rights movement and "Wall Street," or speculative capital, began arriving in Chinatown.

The neighborhood expanded north to Houston Street. Banding together to resist assimilation and racial oppression, the Asian-American movement drew on the antiwar and Black Power movements to forge a shared identity across different Asian ethnicities, producing many of the organizations that exist today in New York, which now range from low-income people power movements to more centrist advocacy groups. Yet at the same time, the real-estate boom, fueled in part by a steady influx of wealthy and middle-class Chinese from Taiwan and Hong Kong, allowed investors to double their investments in just two or three years. Many working-class residents moved out to Brooklyn and Queens, unable to afford rent. Despite some ups and downs, this process of gentrification continues today. Chinatown's revitalized buildings and streets, combined with the myth of the model minority, hide the neighborhood's working poor. Tenant abuse is a daily occurrence in the neighborhood's tenements as landlords seek to convert rent-stabilized buildings into market-rate condominiums. Many work seventy or eighty hours a week, or temporary jobs away from home (a restaurant in Florida for two weeks, or construction work in Virginia) because there is nothing available in New York. Wage-withholding and tip-stealing remain problems as bosses seek to capitalize on the desperation and fear of new immigrants.

So why the conspicuous absence at OWS?

Esther Wang, the director of CAAAV's Chinatown Justice Project (whose members are poor Chinese immigrants), told me that her organization had done community education around OWS and that people understood what it was about. "The question is: what are we going to win from being a part of it? The reality is that these people work like crazy or their situations are highly unstable, so it's hard to plug into a movement that's not accessible and they don't feel welcome."

"It's hard to be a truly multi-racial movement that's inclusive of immigrants. No one knows how to do it yet," she continued. "It's not just about language access, like translating a few articles or documents. It's about language justice."

What this means is crafting messages that speak directly to the realities and needs of Chinatown, and not assuming that the benefits of any "universal" demands we eventually win—say jobs or healthcare for all—will trickle down equally to all. It means shifting the movement's focus from Zuccotti Park to neighborhoods like Chinatown, and working toward economic, social, and racial justice in the poorest and most marginalized communities. Otherwise our claims to true equality are disingenuous—and especially in New York City, whose economy would collapse without the labor of immigrants. "But our attitude isn't that we're going to make this critique and wash our hands of it. We're trying to figure out how to engage people," said Wang. "I think that CAAAV has a responsibility and role to play in thinking about how this can work."

On November 12, CAAAV kicked off an anti-eviction campaign around the building at 11 Allen Street in Chinatown. ("Maybe we'll eventually call it Occupy 11 Allen," joked Wang.) The landlord, who just acquired the building this year, is trying to evict the two-dozen-plus tenants, some of whom have lived there for twenty years. On this Sunday morning, tenants and members gathered before the Skyway Malaysian restaurant on 11 Allen's ground floor as random stragglers waiting for a Chinatown bus watched on. "Down with gentrification!" they shouted in Chinese. Their signs read things like: "Greedy landlords, shame on you!"

Black members of Picture the Homeless spoke about being foreclosed upon—"we all have a right to our homes!"—and their words were translated rapid-fire into Chinese. (The Bronx-based organization has also recently begun to provide some services to the homeless folks at Zuccotti Park.) A young white couple watched from the side, later telling me that they had heard about the event through OWS. Wang says that the campaign might also include a march from Chinatown to Zuccotti Park, where members can teach the Zuccotti-ites about their neighbors: housing and working-class Chinese immigrants.

Maybe Chinatown's low-income workers and residents understand the message of OWS, but does OWS understand anything about Chinatown or what its disparate groups are fighting for? OWS wants inclusivity—hence "the 99 percent"—but what can they bring to a community that has self-organized for over a century against racial discrimination and for economic and social security, without much outside recognition or help? Why should Chinatown jump aboard? Masochism is chasing a self-involved egoist, hoping to be included in their plans and to win their love.

In concrete terms, this means that the OWS should support and participate in immigrant-initiated actions that are in line with our values and principles. There are many. It means initiating dialogue with immigrant communities about how their visions align with ours. If broad transformation is achieved in steps, what steps can we work toward together?

One last thing that occurred to me was that OWS might be inspired by Chinatown's fights, if only they knew about them, just as OWS has now inspired the rest of the world. In 1982, for instance, 20,000 female Chinese garment workers in New York's Chinatown went on strike over plans to reduce wages, holidays, and benefits. They marched through Lower Manhattan to Columbus Park. "When fire singes the hairs on the skin of the women workers, they will rise up like tigers," one of the workers' husbands said. The employers had banked on the movement fracturing over ethnic loyalties, but the women won the first union contracts in the Chinese garment industry. Columbus Park, in the center of Chinatown, is a twenty-minute walk from Zuccotti Park.

It's not that Chinatown doesn't connect with the message of OWS. It's that they've been fighting this fight forever. All the gains they've won, they won themselves. This doesn't mean they won't join us, but neither have we said that we will join them.

STOP STOP-AND-FRISK

SVETLANA KITTO & CELESTE DUPUY-SPENCER

Svetlana Kitto:

The first Stop Stop-and-Frisk action was in Harlem. Thirty-four community members, including Cornel West, blocked the 28th Precinct's entrance and were arrested. The second action was to take place at the 73rd Precinct in Brownsville, Brooklyn. The NYPD policy of stop-and-frisk has been called illegal and unconstitutional by the Center for Constitutional Rights and the New York Civil Liberties Union. It overwhelmingly targets black and Latino men, and only results in arrests five percent of the time. In 2010, there were 600,000 stop-and-frisks in New York. In Brownsville, there are more stop-and-frisks than anywhere else in the city.

On the day of the second action, M. and I walk to the 3 train at Franklin Avenue. It's sunny and cold and there's no evidence of last weekend's snowstorm. M. is planning on getting arrested. When we get to the corner of Rockaway and Livonia, we see a reporter from News 12 setting up her camera in front of the Tilden Projects, also known as the Pink Houses. I cross the street to hand out flyers. People stop in their tracks when I explain to them what we're doing.

"The rally is right across the street," I say. "Then we're marching to the 73rd Precinct."

"Oh no, they don't like me over at the 73rd," a young man with a shaved head says.

One of the organizers is frustrated that more people from the neighborhood aren't coming out. "These people need to stand up. It's their lives being threatened."

My friend Ramdasha disagrees. "People who don't have criminal records, who aren't targeted, are the ones who need to stand up. What would happen if thirty white people blocked a precinct?"

"Maybe this train's the one with all the people," G. says. From the top of the station stairs we can hear drums beating and people chanting, "We won't stop until they stop stop-and-frisk."

SVETLANA KITTO & CELESTE DUPUY-SPENCER

Some of the kids getting off the train are high schoolers who have volunteered to be arrested today. They have on heavy eyeliner and one is wearing a fur hat.

"You guys look great," I say.

"You gotta go out in style," one replies.

It's a little after four and the rally is starting.

"Mic check."

Carl Dix is speaking.

"Stop-and-frisk is unconstitutional, illegal, and racist. Allow me to introduce this generation's Freedom Riders. And some older folks too. Will everyone who is doing civil disobedience please come up?"

The twenty-seven people who are going to be arrested come forward as the crowd falls silent. They look strong, intent, but also scared, like they need our support.

A priest takes the people's mic. "If you think praying to God is going to change this system, you're wrong. Change only happens when the people take it to the streets. Get out of the churches, into the streets."

We begin marching.

Celeste Dupuy-Spencer:

Halfway through the march, Svetlana passes me the corner of the sign she's holding: "From Up Against the Wall to Up in Their Faces." It's five feet tall, the only one of its size, and I feel as though I have suddenly landed a star role in the protest. Quickly, I pass it on. Someone uses a bullhorn, but the batteries are low, so it's not very loud.

"We say no to the new Jim Crow! Stop-and-frisk has got to go!" On Pitkin Avenue, old people sit in chairs under trees and look on as we march past them. Some seem bewildered but others are cheering. A couple of cops walk in the road to keep us on the sidewalk, but we are staying on the sidewalk anyway. I march alongside a young girl and her mother. The girl is obviously excited to be holding her sign, which is almost as tall as she is and reads, "This System Has No Future for the Youth, Revolution Does!" Her mother smiles in encouragement as the girl joins the chant, "Stop-and-frisk don't stop the crime, stop-and-frisk is the crime."

On Bristol Street a young protester points to the building on our right. "There's the juvenile jail. That place is like hell, I know!" He signals to the building to our left: "Here's the 73rd Precinct."

Until now there has been a steady run of conversation. We have been taking note of our comrades and making small talk with people who are, for this moment, friends. But as we approach the precinct, the conversations peter out and together we chant louder than before, over and over, "Cease and desist! Stop stop-and-frisk!"

At Thomas S. Boyland Street and E. New York Avenue, rows of NYPD and Community Affairs officers stand in formation waiting for us. They look ready but not worried. They know the procedure. In front of them metal barricades are arranged into a pen. One of the march organizers cries, "Mic check! Those of you who do not want to be arrested, please stand over there!" He points inside the pen. "Those of you who do plan on being arrested will be walking over to the line of police!" I stand in the pen next to the mother and daughter. A small, older woman with gray hair under her beret grins up at me: "Call me old-fashioned but I have a very hard time believing that it's a good idea to walk into a police pen! This, in my experience, is what I call a trap!" She leaves the pen and scolds the officers as they try to deter her from standing on the sidewalk. The little girl, now perched atop the barricade, drops her mouth wide open as she watches twenty-seven protesters square off with the police. A mass of protesters crowds in from behind, chanting, "We won't stop until we stop stop-and-frisk!" The paddy wagon pulls up. As the chanting continues, the twenty-seven protesters stand in line as, one by one, each is turned around, handcuffed, and escorted to and taken away in a wagon.

We reconvene on the corner. Some guy—possibly hired—agitates and is arrested. The police ask if we need accompaniment to wherever we are marching next. "No! You got to be kidding!" a woman replies. And did I hear a Community Affairs officer call "Mic check"? I did! We march back the way we came.

Before we dispersed, fellow protester Travis Morales made a speech:

> *The sit-ins started in the early sixties down South at the lunch counters with about six people. The Freedom Rides that went down South to register people to vote started with less than fifteen people. But the actions of a few caught the imagination, the inspiration, and support of millions, and Jim Crow segregation and open discrimination, legal discrimination were done away with. And now, though they may tell us that blacks and Latinos are equal before the law, and Commissioner Ray Kelly might tell us that stop-and-frisk is not racial profiling, we have to ask Ray Kelly, "If you say it's not racial profiling, what you been smokin'?" What we have done today is something very special. And our comrades who have gone to jail and put themselves on the line are our heroes. And we need to tell people that! Mic check! I'd like to ask, please raise your hand if you can go back to Occupy Wall Street and spread the word and announce what happened here today.*

All twenty-seven arrested protesters were charged with misdemeanors for obstructing a government agency, fingerprinted and given violations for disorderly conduct. This is a far more serious response than previous arrests, which have either brought no charges or only a violation.

Joanna Neborsky

LABOR, AGAIN

NIKIL SAVAL

Among the endless, nearly bureaucratic proliferation of working groups at Occupy Wall Street and elsewhere—people of color, sanitation, media, alternative banking, sustainability, anti-racism allies, disability—one stands out for its simultaneous universality and total narrowness. The Labor working group, in any occupation, has a very clear and dully unobjectionable task: to help get material support from trade unions for the protests. Usually it consists of people who are union members, who have real but limited ways of getting in touch with their union leadership to encourage them to endorse the various occupations. In this modest task, the Labor working groups have been successful: most trade unions, as well as the largest national labor federation, have serviced the occupations in ways that have helped them sustain themselves over the long haul.

But "labor" means—or should mean—much more than the parlous remainder of American trade unionism. It means "work," and it means "jobs." From Locke, we retain the notion that labor is the source of property, what you put your hands into; from Smith, Ricardo, and Marx, that it is the source of the value of commodities. Labor is the thing one does to sustain life, and the thing that one hates for that very reason; it creates wealth, and it also takes wealth away from the wealthiest.

In the material sense, campaigns for higher wages, employment, sounder trade policies, and a fairer economy have always come from the traditional labor movement. Yet it would fall not to labor but to the short-lived and controversial Demands working group to argue that Occupy Wall Street should enumerate full employment among its chief demands. The renegade methods of the group garnered more discussion than the fact that a (parsimonious) full employment bill already passed as legislation in the 1970s—the Humphrey-Hawkins Full Employment Act—whose impetus and traces of radicalism (mostly expunged by the Chamber of Commerce, which helped to water down the bill) come from the American labor movement, which pushed the hardest for its victory.

I mean to say that the occupations are in danger of treating labor the same way the Democratic Party treats it: as a source of bodies and money, a mere service that tends to be thanked and repudiated in the same breath. Labor, in this way, is like the homeless: it lends legitimacy to but also threatens the burgeoning movement. In a recent *New York Times* article, one protester is quoted as saying, "We're glad to have unions endorse us, but we can't formally endorse them. We're an autonomous group and it's important to keep our autonomy." The protester, like all occupiers, speaks for himself, but for anyone who has heard the discourse on labor coming out of the protests, the comment is emblematic. At one panel discussion in early October, a participant, speaking in the cavalier language of Italian autonomism, derided the efficacy of "union marches." The message is rather clear: Labor unions are welcome to assist the occupations, but they shouldn't expect any help in return. Of course, despite the usual reservations that people have about labor unions and the relegation of issues that should be central to a single, largely unheralded working group, a substantial handful of occupiers have turned out for actions in support of "union marches"—at Sotheby's, Verizon, and elsewhere—much as students in the supposedly hostile New Left did. The same *New York Times* article notes that labor unions have been inspired by the occupations to turn to civil disobedience—a tactic that the labor movement pioneered in the face of much worse violence than flash bombs and tear gas, and which they have in fact continued to practice to this very day. Even the form of the occupation derives in large part, despite or perhaps because of the left's dim memory bank, from the sit-down strike.

In keeping labor unions at a safe distance, the occupations are also in danger of evacuating the concept they have done the most to revive: "solidarity." At another recent panel on Occupy Wall Street, the term came up in a discussion of unions that supported the XL Keystone Pipeline (construction unions, predictably). One panelist argued that we could have "solidarity" with certain institutions without

NIKIL SAVAL

supporting everything they do. But that form of solidarity is just genial condescension. Solidarity—a term that came out of the nascent French labor movement of the 1840s—isn't the same as coalition building: it entails an entire way of life and being in the world, of cementing ties between equals, not a grudging respect between interest groups. In the case of the pipeline, there are several unions (Transit Workers United, Amalgamated Transit Union, Canada's Communications, Energy and Paperworkers Union) that have come out against it. As for the unions that support it, the task of solidarity is not mourning their failure to be as smart as us, but organizing them to be true to shared ideals. Occupiers and those of us who are fellow-travelers cannot act as if we have no obligation to change labor unions to help their goals—as if the one existing institution that has more or less consistently fought for every economic goal they espouse isn't worth transforming, enlarging, and moving.

Photo by Stanley Rogouski

It's worth asking ourselves, on the occupying left, how we plan to reduce inequality without increasing wages; foster employment without cementing the protections against unemployment; ensure that the old retire with dignity without protecting pensions. If there is a single force that has successfully fought for these things besides the labor movement, I'd like to see it. As for their much-despised "bureaucratic" nature, it's hard to see how the occupations—with their teams of lawyers and their masses of committees—have a higher soapbox to stand on.

Recent polls suggest that a majority of Americans would, if given the chance, join a labor union; the same polls suggest that a majority of Americans have an unfavorable view of labor unions. Americans want to have more control over the way they work, but they don't like the form that control tends to take. They like labor, but they hate Labor. This is precisely the paradox that the occupiers face within their own ranks; it indicates a real hostility to an actual problem, but it also suggests that the only way forward is to change that perception. People can endlessly rehearse to themselves the failures of traditional trade unionism, or they can try to change the one available form of organization that promises to deliver the things they want. It has already become customary to speak of the "Occupy movement." But most movements of the past have been clearly for or against something. The antiwar movement. The civil rights movement. The women's liberation movement. The "Occupy movement," which—when it lets its guard down—admits that it wants equality, might do worse than submit to a name that represents the struggle for equality in the past, and call itself a "labor movement."

+ + +

When I volunteered for the local of the hotel workers' union in San Francisco, something I've done on and off for the last two years, there was a contract fight going on, and my job was to get big hotel customers—academic conferences, corporate meetings—not to cross a picket line. Doing so meant first appealing to their sense of solidarity, and then, when that inevitably failed, suggesting that their conference could potentially be ruined by bullhorns and screaming picketers. I had frustrating phone calls with junior academics, who were usually paralyzed by inaction, who wanted to do the right thing that they'd read about in books, but at the crucial moment found themselves constitutionally unable to do the right thing in real life; it was hard for them to see the relationship between their adjunct, benefitless status and the health-care issues facing a hotel worker. On the line outside a hotel, handing out leaflets, I struggled to impress upon a German visitor the fact that a worker's struggle here had relevance to his situation as a worker in Germany. *Genosse*, I started, *Comrade*, taking his hand, but he walked promptly into the hotel.

The young radicals of Silicon Valley were the most disturbing: startup hackers skateboarding through picket lines, covered in piercings and tattoos, praying that tonight would be the night they would get bought out by Microsoft, before investors realized their company had no actual revenue and laid them off. They took our leaflets, crumpled them, and threw them back at us. A tourist from Indiana stopped me for a long conversation about how his furniture company was able to compete with China because it didn't have unions. He paid his employees minimum wage and offered no benefits. As soon as I began to respond with what I knew about China— how badly workers were treated there, how violently the number of labor protests had skyrocketed this year—he shook my hand and walked into the hotel. I pondered the meaning of that handshake as I looked over to see a young man, who looked barely out of college, stopping at the line. He raised his fist and joined the chants; then he asked for some leaflets and started to hand them out. When we asked him why he had joined us, he said, ruefully, that he had just lost his job.

OCCUPY THE BOARD-ROOM

MARK GREIF

On the night that police attacked the Occupy protesters in Oakland, Tuesday, October 25, "non-lethally" fired on them and gassed them and threw stun grenades, and shot in the head an Iraq veteran named Scott Olsen, it looked like our Cub Scout stormtroopers were out to murder American citizens. They aimed high with shotguns at soft-looking Californians in t-shirts and shorts. The organized violence was carried live on KCBS. In the black ant farm chambers of YouTube, I tunneled from one protester video to the next, following morbid links, lying awake in bed in New York. If they were going to destroy the encampments, as was happening simultaneously in Atlanta, and be brutal, as also in Denver and Chicago, then there needed to be new fields opening to occupy. Powerlessness and rage arise from watching suffering at a distance, as in the Age of Television. In the Age of the Internet, links led me back to Occupy the Boardroom, a site that had launched twelve days earlier, and I started writing letters.

The website lists the names of executives and trustees for the big six banks in America: Goldman Sachs, Morgan Stanley, Citigroup, Bank of America, JPMorgan Chase, and Wells Fargo. There are no addresses, not even mailing addresses. But the site is organized to allow you to type a long letter to an individual by name. The service routes your letter to the addressee's email address. It also posts it to a roll of previous letters—more than 6,000, when I first visited—so you learn what other letter-writers know and believe.

> *To: John G Stumpf, Wells Fargo*
> *Thank you for the years of service, But, I am now going to move my money to a Credit Union until I see an effort by the 1 percent to help the country that gave them their chance.*
> *Mr. & Mrs. Anthony Zayas*
> *75234 [Dallas, TX]*

Occupy the Boardroom represents bourgeois protest. I say that as a compliment. I think it's a necessity now, and will be in months to come as mayors try to paint the occupations in the colors of homelessness. Bourgeois protest uses the values of people who hold a stake, who are part of the vast middle class, who are small property owners, or were. The best of America, since Jefferson's vision of yeoman democracy, includes a society of equals in which everyone is an owner of a little bit of the earth to stand on. Occupy Wall Street has, very often, courageously spoken for have-nots, immigrants, and the dispossessed. They're part of America, too. Occupy the Boardroom allows 99 percent of us to speak from principles from which we can never be dispossessed, and from those that, peculiarly, the executives and trustees of banks supposedly share: honesty, probity, contract, politeness, property, savings, professionalism, "customer service," responsibility, citizenship, patriotism. It also lets us speak from everywhere.

To: William R Rhodes, Citigroup

Hello Mr. Rhodes,

I am not poor. In fact, I own a sizeable piece of real estate on the border of Tribeca and the Financial District. I have even paid my mortgage off already.

I am fiscally very conservative. That is why I have no patience for your company's shenanigans.

I have been wanting to leave Citibank for years now. Moving my account from Citi on Nov. 4th is my message to you, and the U.S. Government (1 year out from the election) along with this message here and now.

I am not alone, by the way.

Here's hoping you develop a sense of balance, fairness and a conscience.

Fair thee well,

Heide

[New York, NY]

This matches a new technology to one of the oldest forms enabled by widespread literacy. The individual letter, person to person, secret and intimate or public and formal, but to be read by the recipient in the place appropriate to that

MARK CREIF

communication, on his or her own time, is one of our most protected forms of direct address. Because it is there for the addressee to encounter in calm and security, it is never a trespass if it is polite. Every one of us is *entitled* to be heard in this way by anyone else. It may be a legal offense to tamper with the mail, but it's equally a moral crime to read somebody else's sealed missive or tear open an envelope not addressed to you. What goes unsaid, too, is that *not* reading a personal letter written directly to you is a trespass that leaves us uneasy, an offense against everyone, as uncomfortable as tearing up paper money. It suggests fear, or contempt. To do that, you are putting yourself in the wrong.

> *To: Heidi Miller, JPMorgan Chase*
> *Dear Ms. Miller,*
> *I selected your name from the list of Chase executives listed by the Occupy Wall Street movement because my oldest daughter shares her first name with you and also because I have an account with Chase.*
> *You could say that my wife and I are the lucky ones who are financially secure because we are both retired, have secure retirement Social Security, pensions, and have nest eggs that will survive us both. Our children are also lucky to have relatively secure jobs. But if the decline of our country continues, I am afraid for my grandchildren, perhaps yours too.*
> *But what about the rest of the other 99%? What about our country? Isn't our People the nation for whom our heroes died?*
> *I hope you could be one of the small voices who could also help turn our country around.*
> *Sin cera,*
> *Enrique C. Cubarrubia*

It becomes a way to draw the one percent into the movement, odd as that sounds. It neither tries to co-opt them or vilify them. It addresses them. Politeness may be the most essential thing. "Remember, be polite!" are the words you find in

OCCUPY THE BOARD-ROOM

the text box when you type your letter. "Be sure to" write "in a constructive manner that helps build the movement for a better world. . . . Think funny!" Not many letters are funny. But they are extraordinarily articulate. The politeness is key not because of subservience, and not to charm, but because it assumes community.

> To: *Ellen V Futter, JPMorgan Chase*
>
> *I'm a carpenter, work has been very light since the crash, my wife works in a small factory earning 17 an hour, no insurance. We signed up for "make your home affordable" They reduced our morgage buy 400 a month[,] why we went th[r]ough the process[.] we were not behind in our payments, we just had a hard time makeing ends meet. 9 months into the process they said we were not eligable, that they were going to start forclose if we could not come up with the 400 that we did not pay or we could refi[n]ance at a lower rate saveing us from losing our house and in the process taking all the interest we had paid up to that point ... 10 years 120,000 dollars*
>
> *i know that no one will read this letter but [it] makes me feel better what make[s] you feel better madame*
> *Michael G Anderson*
> *98070 [Vashon, WA]*

MARK CREIF

I confess that I hate it when people's letters are just insults, as some are. Or promises of justice. I do respect it, though—I admire the notes of defiance.

> To: *Diana Taylor, Citigroup*
> *Hi Ms. Taylor:*
> *I have an MBA and work for a large non-profit on the west coast. I'm involved only recently in politics, and I have learned a bit since 2008.*
> *Consider what you could do instead with all the money your company currently contributes to various political campaigns & lobbying groups.*

You could make more small business loans, and create jobs and help local economies. You could maintain your profits without having to layoff people.
You could take your chances competing without stacking the deck by influencing favorable legislation.
Flavia Franco
94403 [San Mateo, CA]

"But none of the bankers are going to read the letters!" one of my family members said. I'm reading them, I said. Other letter-writers are reading mine. Now we all see each other. "But the letters are never even going to be opened by the people to whom they're written!" I'm not sure of that, I said. Mightn't they be?

+ + +

Needless to say, I was pretty excited when I read that Occupy the Boardroom would be rallying on the steps of the New York Public Library on Friday, October 28, to deliver the letters to banks.

The familiar techniques of the people's mic were used to let people tell stories about school debt, hospital bills, and tiny loans that ballooned as jobs were lost. I went with the group that marched to Bank of America, since that's my bank. I have been with them for more than a decade, ever since they bought the bank that bought the bank that sits on a corner in my hometown.

We marched down 42nd Street. The plan was to go to Wells Fargo after we had a media moment at the Bank of America headquarters on Sixth Avenue, and then Chase. The organizers had asked if anyone wanted to carry the letters personally, and I did—hoping this would mean I'd get to go inside and see how they planned to get these to people's desks. I had a box filled with several hundred printed letters. I wondered if I'd get to say something noble as I handed them over. I imagined myself like one of the Founders, in a periwig, and I was d88988 hi198

MARK GREIF

mentally rehearsing: "You, sir—" and polite but Jacobin remarks, and appeals to humility. We were encouraged to hand out individual letters to people who passed by, and I had to stop to explain what was happening, first to an oddball with a microphone and then to a schoolkid doing a report.

That made me late crossing the avenue, and thus left out. There were pirates up front—representing corporate pirates?—and group chanting. There was an avalanche of police, a hundred or more, for protesters who didn't number more than 300, and then the fact that the police had set up inside the Bank of America Tower perimeter—behind barriers they had set out on the pavement, such that they had made themselves the house security of the bank—seemed to mean we wouldn't be hand-delivering letters, nor even leaving them all in a sack in the lobby. Bank employees stared from behind the glass. It was a sunny day, cold and very peaceful.

Because I was at the back, I saw that close to where I was standing was an opening in the barricade, where the NYPD was talking to folks in a line. I thought I'd give them letters. My logic was that standers on line are more likely to accept reading material than folks you interrupt as they're moving. My patter was: "Can I offer you a letter from an individual American citizen to employees of Bank of America?" starting at the end of the line.

"No," said my first try.

"OK," I said. Moving on, "Can I offer you a letter?" From an individual American citizen, etc.

This man was completely silent. He and I were standing still, at a distance of social comfort, had calm voices, relaxed postures. He was avoiding my eye. An offer in that situation just about always dictates a spoken "no," unless there's some reason to perceive a threat.

Oh! A dim light dawned. "Are you guys by any chance employees of Bank of America?"

"No," the first man said. Which provoked a reaction like a slap in the face of the second one, because it meant that his comrade had outright lied.

They were all employees, reentering the bank. At the head of the line were uniformed NYPD, working for the in-house Bank of America security, checking ID. So I started working the line. "Sir, can I offer you these letters from fellow American citizens? *They're addressed to you.*"

The people waiting reflected the usual breakdown of decency, shyness, and bad personalities. The surprise was a knot of eager Columbia Business School students. They refused to take letters, until one did, and then they all did.

Meanwhile, I missed the formal protest. On the other side of the police barrier stood a line of thirty or forty blue-uniformed police, backs against the glass front of the Bank of America Tower as if guarding a jewelry exhibit, with thirty feet of barricaded-off open pavement which the protesters now filled with a flotilla of paper planes. The original idea had been to write new letters and launch them as a publicity stunt. Absent time to write these, and with no way now to deliver the real letters, people had started using the printouts to make the planes. Everyone then picked up the ones that had blown back onto their side, brushed off any dirt, and moved down 42nd Street to head for Wells Fargo, where the next round of boxes was due for delivery. My trouble was, I still had so many letters. So I went back to quickly try to hand them out to people at the police gate.

With most people gone, I saw that in-house security called out a team of janitors to sweep up the letters, lying there in the form of paper planes, and dump them in a big gray trash can. I went to the security—five men in suits, who were not bankers—and leaned over the barricade to address the one giving orders. "Hey, these are letters from individual American citizens, and you're treating them like trash." Nothing doing. "Listen, let me pick up the letters, I'll do it for your guys. Then I'll have the letters, and nobody's letter has to be thrown out."

"YOU CAN'T COME IN HERE!" So he heard me.

"How about this—you have your guys, can they just give them to me—I'll stay on this side—dump them with me, instead of the trash, and I'll clean them up?" Back to pretending.

"How come you can't talk to me?" I said. "Is it a legal thing, or are you afraid to? Or do you just not like me?"

"*I* don't like you!" a banker jeered as he passed through the barricade.

"That's OK, I'm your customer," I said.

It was depressing. The janitors came and did the public sidewalk around me, all three Latino, workers for sub-contracting companies, by the patches on their shirts, presumably so the bank wouldn't have to employ them and pay benefits. "I'm with you, man, hey, sorry, man. I got to keep my job, if I was off work, I'd be out here with you."

I felt fake, because, in class and privileges, I have plenty in common with those people standing in line to go to their jobs in the bank. I'm a college teacher, well-employed. Any of us employed has it easier than the unemployed, whose stories were in these letters that I kept glancing down at, each one different. My father works for a bank, in Boston, developing their computer systems. I have health benefits, and also the arrogance that comes from fancy degrees, the feeling of comfort and ownership at the library and the museum, that nobody ranks above me except the super-rich (and great artists and writers).

And surely I know how we think—and how the people who work in banks, like my father and his coworkers, think—and school friends, and friends' spouses, who work in the banks, in finance, how they think, and, yes, some of us are assholes, but mostly it's still people with a moral core. The agenda of normalcy and reputation just happens to be what's current with the folks around us. If you spend all your time with bankers, you will think that some things that are wrong are actually OK. We live in bubbles. If a message can get across that barrier, just to say *what is coming from your work is not what you believe in, it's a national horror*, people will surely change. Won't they?

MARK CREIF

SCENES FROM OCCUPIED ATLANTA

KUNG LI

Occupy Wall Street and its offshoots have been catching flak for being so white. Occupy Atlanta is no exception, getting off to a rough start last Friday when civil rights movement hero-turned-Congressman John Lewis stopped by to offer his support, only to be waved off by the mostly white General Assembly. Congressman Lewis was extremely gracious. Others, less so.

In a town that is majority black, Occupy Atlanta moved quickly to make amends. The occupiers renamed their camp-site Troy Davis Park on Sunday, October 9, in honor of what would have been Troy Davis's forty-third birthday. They apologized, explaining that the democratic process of ordering speakers is crucial to the movement. They extended an invitation to John Lewis to return.

Getting it right about race is important for the Occupy movement everywhere, but especially here in Georgia, where there is nothing subtle about the relationship between race, corporations and the government. Georgia's government was created by and for plantation farmers, the original one percent, running antebellum corporations. And that one percent has been using everything in its power, most notably the criminal justice system, to hold onto its centuries-old gains.

Occupy Atlanta is still braving the elements today in Woodruff Park, a green space in the middle of downtown Atlanta. Many in and around the Occupy movement have been asking how we can talk about corporate control of government, economics, and race all in the same breath. Considering the history of Woodruff Park, we have to wonder how we can talk about it any other way. Here, I offer a crucial primer for the full history of this occupied space.

Occupied Atlanta, 1865

When the Georgia Legislature convened after the Civil War, it dutifully ratified the Thirteenth Amendment, as it was required to do to reenter the Union. The Thirteenth Amendment abolished slavery, except as punishment for crime.

With the amendment ratified, the all-white Georgia Legislature passed the Black Codes, effectively reinstating slavery in Georgia. The Codes required former slaves to enter into labor contracts, with wages to be paid by the master totaling—after deductions for food, shelter, and penalties for days not worked—two cents an hour. That's how Georgia's antebellum one percent had rolled before the war, and that's how they wanted to roll after it. The only industry had been cotton, so the Black Codes were written to keep freedmen working the same fields they had worked as slaves.

Those who resisted this reenslavement were confronted by a new vagrancy law; the enforcement of the Black Codes that made it illegal to "wander or stroll about in idleness" without a labor contract. Joseph Brown was arrested on Decatur Street in 1868, one of hundreds. Rather than picking cotton under a labor contract, he was in Atlanta without work. The charge: vagrancy.

Mr. Brown and other freedmen who were sentenced as vagrants were not sent to prison. Georgia's prison had been burned during the war, and there was no money to rebuild. Rather, they were leased out to plantation owners, railroad companies, and coal mines. Georgia's first lease-off in 1868 was to a railroad company: $2,500 bought 100 black men, arrested for vagrancy or loitering and forced to work not as slaves but as convicts.

This was the start of the modern criminal justice system. It was started, you might say, right here where Occupy Atlanta will be sleeping tonight, in Woodruff Park, by the post–Civil War plantation owners intent on keeping the work of black men and women cheap and available.

Occupied Atlanta, 1906

In 1906, Decatur Street, where Mr. Brown had been arrested thirty-eight years earlier, was now lined with saloons, hotels, a buggy repair shop, and the post office.

SCENES FROM OCCUPIED ATLANTA

In spring of that year, the Chief of Police in Atlanta launched a campaign to rid the city of black men. He committed a full squad of officers to "arrest all loafers" and close down the "negro dives" that lined Decatur Street in downtown Atlanta. The chief told City Council that in order to arrest and prosecute all the vagrants, he would need fifty additional policemen.

Pressure to "arrest and lock up all the negroes who were idling about the city" intensified through the summer and into the fall. By the third week in September, coverage about the police campaign against "vagrants" and "negro dives" merged into sensational stories about white women around the city fending off sexual attacks by black men. Four such allegations turned into front page headlines in that week in September. On Saturday night, thousands of white men gathered in Five Points, sent there by the newspapers exhorting "good white men" to band together and take action to protect their women from "black beasts" and "animals."

By the time the sun set, over 5,000 white men were milling around Five Points. They were stomping their feet on the ground where Occupy Atlanta's general assemblies sit. Their numbers doubled over the next two hours, men armed with rifles, pistols, long knives and clubs. They were ready to kill.

And kill they did. Groups of twenty, thirty, 100 burst forward in a sprinting chase whenever a black man or boy appeared. A footrace up Peachtree Street, another down Decatur Street, another across a bridge flying over the railroad tracks. Three bodies were dumped in a pile at the foot of the statue of Henry Grady on Marietta Street. A black man was strung up on a lamppost along Peachtree. The white mobs raged through the night, quieting in the early morning.

Over three days, twenty-five black Atlantans were killed, maybe more. Another fifty or more had injuries serious enough to brave the streets to get to Grady Hospital. There is neither memorial nor mention of the dead among the commemorations in Woodruff Park.

KUNG LI

Occupied Atlanta, 1960

Half a century later, the streets here around Woodruff Park had been scrubbed clean of any reminder of the race riot. Where the saloons had been were now office buildings—some modern steel frame, some red brick.

On February 1, 1960, four black students in Greensboro, N.C., sat down at a Woolworth lunch counter and waited to be served. The police came but could not arrest the students because they were not breaking any law. The next day, the students returned and again sat quietly at the Woolworth lunch counter. The media picked up the story, and the sit-ins spread. On February 13, 500 students in Nashville sat-in at lunch counters across the city.

The Georgia Legislature responded with astonishing speed, passing a new trespassing law four days later—should the sit-ins spread to Atlanta, they wanted a law that would let the police make arrests. A small law would do. Cast in the same mold as the early-century vagrancy laws, the new trespass law made it a crime to remain on the premises after being asked to leave.

In October, Atlanta students staged mass demonstrations and sit-ins at the Rich's Department Store in downtown Five Points and other counters across the city. Two blocks south of Woodruff Park, where occupiers will sleep tonight, black students trained in nonviolent direct action took an elevator up to Rich's sixth-floor Magnolia Room, or down to the Cockrel Grill in the basement, then sat down and waited to be served.

Occupied Atlanta, 1996

Atlanta changed. Rich's downtown became Macy's. A slain King made a final journey through the streets of Atlanta in a wooden farm wagon drawn by two mules before being laid to rest in South View Cemetery. The students who had been arrested for trespassing became fathers, nurses, elected officials.

Then in 1996, the Olympics came to Atlanta. The city built a new jail in record time; it was the first facility completed

SCENES FROM OCCUPIED ATLANTA

for the Games. The city also closed down Woodruff Park and renovated it. The city took its time—it was their best chance to move out the homeless men and women who slept in the park—and when the park was reopened, it had been landscaped with a wide open slope to make it easier for police to keep it clear of the visibly poor.

Officials with the Atlanta Olympic Committee insisted the police were not used to clear poor black people out of downtown Atlanta for the Games. Yet, the visibly poor—nearly all black—disappeared from Woodruff Park for the duration of the Games. The county jail's population shot up from 2,200 to 4,500 before and during the Olympics. Officials insisted: just a coincidence.

Should the Atlanta Police decide to evict Occupy Atlanta from Woodruff Park, they will likely use one of the ordinances banning overnight sleeping or camping on public space, passed before and immediately after the 1996 Olympics.

Occupied Atlanta, 2011

Five days before the execution of Troy Davis, thousands of Atlantans gathered at Woodruff Park to march to Ebenezer Baptist Church for a part-vigil, part-protest that recalled the civil rights movement's most raucous mass meetings. The protest was majority—an overwhelming majority, if you include those already seated in Ebenezer Church—African American. The State of Georgia was not moved and proceeded to kill Troy Davis by lethal injection. Occupy Atlanta is majority—at times an overwhelming majority—white. It is trying to figure out how to do right by race.

But being anti-racist in this place—that is, in Woodruff Park, in Atlanta, in Georgia, in the South—is not mainly about getting more people of color to pitch a tent and sleep out there. Truth be told, I'm kind of OK with having mostly white people sleeping out there, because when the junta that runs downtown Atlanta decides it has had enough and people get carted off to jail, there's no need to have more black or brown people in the Atlanta City Detention Center.

Being anti-racist is: if you are going to set up camp and take Five Points as your center point, acknowledging that the corporate forces at play around there are totally about race. This is true currently, and it is true historically—no surprise. When Occupy Wall Street declared, "We come to you at a time when corporations, which place profit over people, self-interest over justice, and oppression over equality, run our governments," that was old news here, friends. The plantation owners have always run Georgia's government.

But they have not always run the street. In 1960, the students won. Was it because they were one sit-in among dozens of sit-ins happening around the country, much like Occupy Atlanta is one of dozens? Was it because they had both strong process and direct action? Was it because they confronted the criminal justice system head on, demanding to be arrested and refusing to post bail? Maybe, maybe, maybe.

SCENES FROM OCCUPIED ATLANTA

Illustration by Erin Schell. Police Photo by Michael Gould-Wartofsky

(UN) OCCUPY

ANGELA DAVIS

Remarks at Washington Square Park, October 30

We challenge language. We transform language. We remain aware of all of the resonances of the language we use. We know that the movement in Puerto Rico is raising the slogan "(Un)Occupy." We must be aware when we say "Occupy Wall Street" that this country was founded on the genocidal occupation of indigenous lands. We must be aware when we say "Occupy Wall Street" or "Occupy Washington Square" that occupations in other countries are violent and brutal. Palestine remains occupied territory, and we have to learn how to say "no" to military occupations. At the same time, we transform the meaning of "occupation." We turn "occupation" into something that is beautiful, something that brings community together. Something that calls for love and happiness and hope.

(UN)OCCUPY

SCENES FROM OCCUPIED OAKLAND

SUNAURA TAYLOR

October 17

I just woke up in my tent at Occupy Oakland. This is the first night my husband and I (and our dog) have camped out here, and though I can't say we slept well over the sounds of the city and people talking into the early hours of the morning, we woke up still deeply enthused and excited to be part of such an event in Oakland.

We've been stopping by the encampment since it started last Monday. It's in downtown Oakland, in Frank Ogawa Plaza, which is right in front of the city hall. Within hours of the protest starting, there were signs renaming the location. The new name: Oscar Grant Plaza.

Frank H. Ogawa was a Japanese American who was a longtime Oakland City Council member. He had served time during WWII in a concentration camp. He died while the plaza was being renovated, and so it was named in his honor. Oscar Grant was a young African-American man who was fatally shot by BART (Bay Area Rapid Transit) police on New Year's Day 2009. The shooting, which made headlines nationwide, has become a symbol of the city's problem of police brutality and racial inequality. The movement for justice that has emerged from Oscar Grant's shooting has no doubt played a powerful role in how Occupy Oakland has been organized.

It was clear from the first signs that went up at the encampment, and the first organizers who spoke, that Oscar Grant Plaza was going to be as much about addressing and healing Oakland's wounds as it was about uniting the 99 percent. This was not going to be an encampment that ignored issues of race, class, nationality and gender, and as I've found out over the past few days, in at least some ways, they've also been trying to address issues of disability.

Although I'm the only wheelchair user I've seen staying at the camp (which doesn't mean I necessarily am the only one here), the Bay Area's disability community has been coming out to support the events and participate in the protest. This weekend over 2,500 people made it to Oscar Grant Plaza for a march and rally calling for "Jobs Not Cuts." Among the protesters were many individuals from various unions, including SEIU. CUIDO, a radical activist group made up of disabled people and allies, was also present. CUIDO—which stands for Communities United in Defense of Olmstead (a landmark court decision that declared that disabled people have a right to live in their own communities)—is no stranger to protest encampments. In the summer of 2010, dozens of members of CUIDO camped out in tents on a median in Berkeley to protest the proposed budget cuts to services that are heavily relied upon by the poor, elderly, and disabled folks. Arnieville (named after our then Governor Arnold Schwarzenegger) was a remarkably accessible tent city and thrived for over a month.

Although Oscar Grant Plaza has yet to be as accessible to a broad range of disabled people as Arnieville, I've been pleasantly surprised by how an awareness of disability has been at least somewhat present over the past week. Ableism was mentioned during the General Assembly meeting as an issue that the Safe Place working group wanted to address, and I've seen signs for "access for all," demanding people keep ramps clear.

Still, seven days into the protest there is no longer any room for tents on the plaza's large lawn. Tents are squeezed together so tightly that in many areas there is no room to move in between them, for me in my wheelchair or for someone who walks. There is more access to the community tents. There is a free school, an art station, a Sukkot tent, a medical tent, a children's area, a people of color tent, and a quite remarkable food station, where huge batches of soups and beans are made, and tea, coffee, and healthy snacks seem to be abundant. The various projects the camp is working on include installing solar panels and reclaiming parts of the park as a community garden.

One of the most amazing aspects of being at Oscar Grant Plaza is witnessing how moved people are. People who may never have said a word to each other a week ago are now neighbors. The General Assembly meetings, which happen every evening, are often very beautiful. Of course people bicker, or

SUNAURA TAYLOR

get bored, or are sometimes disrespectful, but much of the time the meetings are thoughtful and patient.

The assembly talked very vulnerably about how to deal with sexism and violence at the campsite. We talked about the complexity of discouraging certain behaviors like drinking and partying, while also trying to respect people's individual freedoms. There was a strong sense of support, of watching out for each other, and of not wanting to give the police or the city any reason to try to kick us out. The Security working group, which enlists volunteers to take shifts watching out for the campers throughout the night, encouraged more people to sign up.

Negotiating what different people want for the atmosphere of the camp is undoubtedly a challenge. Some of the protesters seem adamant that there can't be a revolution without a rocking party, while others repeated numerous times that although they weren't strangers to partying themselves, "This camp is not Burning Man!"

Participating in this movement is intimidating in many ways, especially for people who are shy, or those who feel that there is no one "like them" at the protests. I'm certainly intimidated by camping with strangers, by being one of the only visibly disabled people present, and by the lack of access and simple comforts. However, I want to be out there, because I realize that this sort of opportunity to come together doesn't happen every day. But also, I want to be there because I am hella proud of Oakland for creating this sort of encampment— an encampment that often fails in its desire to be a safe and accessible place for all people, but that is nonetheless trying.

October 27

Early Tuesday morning, Occupy Oakland encampments at Oscar Grant Plaza and Snow Park were raided and destroyed by police. There were numerous reports of excessive use of force and violence. Nearly 100 people were arrested and held on $10,000 bail. The emergency text alert system, which apparently had over 1,000 people signed on, failed to go off for many of us, and so occupiers were left alone to defend the camps in the early hours of the morning. The police blocked off streets, rerouted buses, and shut down the closest BART stop. Because of the police blockade, it was reportedly next to impossible for media or legal observers to witness events. Photos from the raided Oscar Grant Plaza show an utterly destroyed encampment, with tents cut up and intentionally destroyed.

At 4 PM that day, people who had not been arrested, as well as supporters of Occupy Oakland, rallied at the Oakland public library to show support of those arrested and outrage over the destruction of the camps. What began as a rally and march of about 500 people turned into a march of thousands. We marched through Oakland reclaiming our streets and demanding our parks be returned to us. Over and over again, we were met with tear gas and extreme police force. Many people were injured, including Scott Olsen, a twenty-four-year-old veteran who survived two deployments to Iraq. He was hit in the head with a police projectile (either a tear-gas canister or a flash-bang grenade) and was in critical condition up until last night when he was downgraded to serious but stable condition. Videos show that as protesters rushed in to help the man, police threw another tear-gas canister or flash-bang grenade at them. One photo shows a woman in a wheelchair, a member of CUIDO, in a cloud of tear gas. The energy, although often very scary, was amazing—passionate and brave and dedicated. The protesters vowed to be out there every evening at 6 PM until our parks were reclaimed.

As the world turned its attention to Oakland, my partner and I had to leave, taking the red eye out that night to New York for a family engagement. The next day we were both glued to the reports of the amazing rally that took place that night. Three thousand people reclaimed Oscar Grant Plaza, tearing down (and neatly stacking) the fence that the police had used to encircle the camp. The police stood back as a general assembly of nearly 1,600 people voted on proposals of what to do next. The general assembly passed a decision to have a general strike and mass day of action on Wednesday, November 2.

November 2

I had no idea a movement could grow so quickly. On October 25, Oscar Grant Plaza was raided and destroyed by riot cops. Only a week and a half later, you never would have known it had gone. The tent city has been resurrected.

Occupy Oakland is not even a month old and yet it has become an incredible force in this city. It held the nation's first general strike in over sixty-five years (the last general strike was also held in Oakland in 1946). Thousands of people came. The exact numbers are unclear, but it seems likely it was between 5,000–10,000 people, although some estimates put it anywhere from 20,000–40,000. The day was glorious and peaceful (even the mayor and the city council members had to admit it was remarkable). Unfortunately, it ended in the yellow fog of nighttime tear gas and police violence.

The strike was a huge success, with a sustained energy from the early morning hours until the late hours of the night. Multiple banks were forced to close throughout the day and a massive march and sit-in during the evening hours shut down the Port of Oakland. For the whole day and into the night, protesters occupied 14th Street and Broadway, the main intersection beside the encampment. Huge handmade banners hung across roads and in front of banks declaring things like "Death to Capitalism." The intersection and the camp itself was the central hub of the protest, but throughout the day groups of hundreds or thousands would leave, march across Oakland to a bank or to participate in an action or event, while thousands of others stayed at Oscar Grant Plaza, to dance, make political signs, and celebrate. Hot food was provided and cooked by local businesses, union representatives, firefighters, occupiers, and countless others. The atmosphere was festival-like, but only better, as everyone seemed to be talking about changing the world—and actually believing in it. Even by night, after sitting at the port in the cold for many hours, people still seemed overjoyed. One person told me it was the best day of his life.

People had been urged throughout the days leading up to the event to organize their own actions, and that's clearly what happened. Everywhere you went you'd find different pockets of people self-organizing. From the Children's Brigade to the Disability Action Brigade, to a flash mob singing "I will Survive (Capitalism)," to a 99% storytelling tent, countless groups of people made their own creative and powerful moments of resistance.

At the port we split into groups, each blocking a separate entrance. At 7 PM a new work shift was going to begin and we were to block the workers from entering by creating massive community picket lines. This action had largely been developed to show solidarity with the Longshore Workers in Longview, WA, who have been battling EGT (Export Grain Terminal) for months over anti-union practices. Many Longshore Workers announced solidarity with the strike, even as the International Longshore and Warehouse Union was unable to officially authorize it. Although there were reports of some frustrated truckers (and two marchers were injured by an angry driver), the vast majority honked their horns enthusiastically in support of us and some even let protesters climb atop their containers for a better view of the seemingly endless parade of people. Spontaneous general assemblies were held at each gate using the human microphone, where a lot of conversation seemed to focus on the importance of occupying foreclosed spaces, especially as winter nears. After many hours it was announced that we had successfully shut down the Port of Oakland. My partner and I cheered and then began the long march back.

The cops were largely absent despite a few incidents of property damage to some banks and a Whole Foods grocery store. A small number of protesters smashed windows, broke ATMs, and spray-painted messages on the outside of banks.

SUNAURA TAYLOR

YouTube videos show other protesters trying to stop the vandalism, sometimes with force. People debated the vandalism throughout the day—with many staunchly opposed to it, and others arguing that property damage isn't violence (what the banks do is violence). Still others argued that, either way, these tactics are unhelpful and turn people away from the movement. After the police violence of the week before, which drew international attention and which left people hurt, it was clear that the city of Oakland did not want any more bad press. However, as the night wore on things began to change.

When my partner and I arrived back at Oscar Grant Plaza, exhausted and ready for our second night at the new camp, we were told that a group of protesters had occupied a nearby foreclosed building and that the police were coming. It is hard to know what exactly happened before or after the police raid, but within twenty minutes hundreds of cops in full riot gear had descended on Occupy Oakland and were blasting the crowds with tear gas. I felt confused by what was going on, as I had left the port with no knowledge that a building occupation had been planned. Later large fires were lit by some of the protesters (supposedly to combat the tear gas), and some bottles were hurled at the cops.

I can't stop thinking about what happened that night. Besides being disheartened once again by the brutality of the cops (who, along with tear gas, shot rubber bullets at people, one of which hit a homeless man), I also felt dismayed and betrayed by some of the protest activity itself. As I watched from a distance it seemed to me that the crowd was largely very young and very able-bodied. It is easy for me to assume they were also predominantly white and male (since I was not on the frontlines, I'm not sure). I do know, though, that as a disabled woman and wheelchair user, I felt little of the diversity of people that makes this movement so beautiful and so revolutionary to me.

As I've watched the debate unfold it seems that one of the main points of contention is over whether or not destruction of property is violence. In my opinion destruction of property has had its place even within nonviolent movements, but it is a tactic that too often is used rashly and dangerously. After all, the one percent were not the ones out in the streets of Oakland the next morning sweeping up the shattered glass or picking up the burned debris. I do think there is a kind of violence in the way property destruction affects others without their consent. A small group of people making decisions that affect the safety and reputation of the whole movement is not what democracy looks like. That is what violence looks like.

However, the violence perpetrated by the protestors was minimal compared to the violence perpetrated by the police in response. Yet again a person was seriously injured, and bizarrely, it was another young Iraq war veteran, Kayvan Sabeghi, who was walking alone when he was stopped by a group of cops who proceeded to beat him with batons. Kayvan was in jail for eighteen hours calling for help and in excruciating pain. When he finally got to the hospital, doctors discovered that his spleen had been ruptured.

I awoke at my home on November 3 and was incredibly relieved to hear that the camp had not been destroyed; I was also relieved to see that the media coverage of the violence had not completely overshadowed all the spectacular moments of the day. The day of the general strike proved that there are thousands, if not tens of thousands, of people who support Occupy Oakland. To me, the only thing the broken windows, spray paint, and fires have done thus far is make some groups, small businesses, and unions more hesitant to support us, and it has made many individuals feel less safe.

The evening after the strike, Occupy Oakland held a forum on violence and nonviolence. Occupy Oakland supports a diversity of tactics, but as one woman said at the forum, respecting a diversity of tactics must go both ways. When a few people choose violence, they need to be aware of how their tactics can trump the tactics of those who choose nonviolence. I would hate to see this movement slowed down or destroyed by infighting. I'd also hate to see it fall apart

SUNAURA TAYLOR

because of violence. To me, it's essential that we really think complexly about what respecting a diversity of tactics—and a diversity of people—really means. Our future depends on it.

November 13

On November 10, as Oscar Grant Plaza prepared to celebrate its one-month anniversary, a young man was shot and killed a few yards away. While the tragic event has engendered many responses—from those who have used it as a justification to evict the campers, to others who say that this sort of tragedy is nothing new to Oakland—it cannot be disconnected from the systemic issues that the Occupy movement is protesting. The Occupy Oakland medics were the first to respond on the scene. As one of them, a young black man, said later, "I have been to seventy-nine funerals in my twenty-two years of life. This is what happens in Oakland." Later other people made the point that if a young black man is shot in Oakland it usually never makes the news.

I am young, female, a wheelchair user, and I am white. I have had an intense education in the past month on what my city is really like for much of its population—and it is devastating. The very first day Oscar Grant Plaza was erected people yelled, "Fuck the cops!" and it was made clear this was not a space that would welcome or negotiate with police. I remember thinking, "That is too bad. We should give the cops a chance." I have learned over the past few weeks just how privileged that sentiment was.

I have been arrested twice in my life, both times with a relatively small group of disabled people. Both times the police for the most part were careful and polite, albeit clearly patronizing (this is not always the case, as police violence against disabled people is actually quite common). What I have seen the cops do to Occupy Oakland, Occupy Cal and countless other occupations across the country, is nothing short of criminal. The cops are not polite and careful if you are homeless, if you are poor, if you are a person of color. The cops are not polite and careful if you are part of a movement that they understand as actually threatening to change the status quo.

I have seen video of police brutally beating students at UC Berkeley with batons, pulling their hair and jabbing them forcefully in the stomach. I've been a short distance away from them as they shot tear gas into spaces they knew included children, disabled people, homeless people, and animals. I've seen footage and read stories of officers shamelessly shooting rubber bullets at people, including those with cameras. Across the country in dozens of locations the cops are surrounding, destroying, and brutalizing protesters. From Occupy Atlanta to Occupy Salt Lake City, from Occupy Denver to Occupy Portland, police are attacking our cities. It is hard to believe these are just isolated instances. It seems much more like a national organized attack on the movement.

This type of brutality is new to many of us. Like me, many people were surprised by the level of violence the cops have used. But to many communities in Oakland this is simply more of the same. I will now have much more understanding for those who yell, "Fuck the cops!" even if I choose not to yell this myself. I am ashamed I was so naïve about the cops in Oakland, but even more than this I am furious. I am furious that the police are allowed to brutalize people without being held accountable for their actions. Even more than this, police violence needs to be publicly disgraced as the unlawful, unjust, and corrupt tactic that it is. As Occupy Oakland braces for another raid and undergoes a barrage of criticism (some valid, but much not) over the violent tactics a few protesters have used, the police force that has hurt, maimed, and nearly killed numerous protesters has slipped by with little more damage than a bit of bad press.

But more than this, I am outraged that police violence makes these protests so unsafe that many of us who are more vulnerable cannot even exercise our right to protest, whether our vulnerabilities stem from age, immigration status, illness, or disability. Every time I go down to Oscar Grant Plaza now, I weigh the risks I take on as a disabled person who can't run away, a person who can't cover my mouth or my eyes if they lob tear gas at me. This makes me furious, because I have just as much right to voice my dissent as anyone else.

Sunaura Taylor, "Corporate Welfare"

THROWING OUT THE MASTER'S TOOLS AND BUILDING A BETTER HOUSE

REBECCA SOLNIT

Violence Is Conventional

Violence is what the police use. It's what the state uses. If we want a revolution, it's because we want a better world, because we think we have a bigger imagination, a more beautiful vision. So we're not violent; we're not like them in crucial ways. When I see a New York City policeman pepper-spray already captive young women in the face, I am disgusted; I want things to be different. And that pepper-spraying incident, terrible though it was for the individuals, did not succeed in any larger way.

In fact, seen on YouTube (three quarters of a million times for one posted version) and widely disseminated, it helped make Occupy Wall Street visible and sympathetic to mainstream viewers. The movement grew tremendously after that. The incident demonstrated the moral failure of the police and demonstrated that violence is also weak. It can injure, damage, destroy, kill, but it can't coerce the will of the people, whether it's a policeman assaulting unarmed young women or the US Army in Vietnam or Iraq.

Imagine that some Occupy activists had then beaten up the cop. That would have seemed to justify him in the eyes of many; it would have undermined the moral standing of our side. And then what? Moral authority was also that young Marine veteran, Shamar Thomas, chewing out thirty or so New York cops in what became a YouTube clip viewed over two and a half million times so far. He didn't fight them; he told them that what they were doing was wrong and dishonorable. And brought the nation along with him. Which violence wouldn't do.

Violence Is Weak

As Jonathan Schell points out in his magnificent book *The Unconquerable World: Power, Nonviolence, and the Will of the People*, violence is what the state uses when its other powers have failed, when it is already losing. In using violence the state often loses its moral authority and its popular support.

That's why sometimes their visible violence feeds our victory, tragic though the impact may be. It's also telling that when the FBI or other government agencies infiltrate a movement or an activist group, they seek to undermine it by egging it on to more violence.

The state would like us to be violent. Violence as cooptation tries to make us more like them, and if we're like them they win twice—once because being unlike them is our goal and again because then we're easier to imprison, brutalize, marginalize, etc. We have another kind of power, though the term *nonviolence* only defines what it is not; some call our power *people power*. It works. It's powerful. It has changed and is changing the world.

The government and mainstream-to-right media often like to create fictions of our violence, from the myth that protesters were violent (beyond property damage) in Seattle in 1999, to the myth of spitting in returning soldiers' faces in the Vietnam era, to generally smearing us as terrorists. If we were violent, we would be conventionally dangerous and the authorities could justify repressing us. In fact, we're unconventionally dangerous, because we're not threatening physical violence but the transformation of the system (and its violence). That is so much more dangerous to them, which is why they have to lie about (or just cannot comprehend) the nature of our danger.

So when episodes of violence break out as part of our side in a demonstration, an uprising, a movement, I think of it as a sabotage, a corruption, a coercion, a misunderstanding, or a mistake, whether it's a paid infiltrator or a clueless dude. Here I want to be clear that property damage is not necessarily violence. The firefighter breaks the door to get the people out of the building. But the husband breaks the dishes to demonstrate to his wife that he can and may also break her; it is violence displaced onto the inanimate as a threat to the animate.

Quietly eradicating experimental GMO crops or pulling up mining claim stakes is generally like the firefighter. Breaking windows during a big demonstration is more like the husband.

I saw the windows of a Starbucks and a Niketown broken in downtown Seattle after nonviolent direct action had shut down the central city and the World Trade Organization ministerial. I saw scared-looking workers and knew that the CEOs and shareholders were not going to face that turbulence, and they sure were not going to be the ones to clean it up. Economically, it meant nothing to them.

We Are Already Winning

The powers that be are already scared of the Occupy movement, and not because of tiny acts of violence. They are scared because right now we speak pretty well for the 99 percent. And because we set out to change the world, and it's working. At the G20 Summit in November, Russian president Dmitry Medvedev warned, "The reward system of shareholders and managers of financial institutions should be changed step by step. Otherwise the 'Occupy Wall Street' slogan will become fashionable in all developed countries." That's fear. And capitulation. *New York Times* columnist Paul Krugman opened a recent column thus: "Inequality is back in the news, largely thanks to Occupy Wall Street." We have set the agenda and framed the terms, and that's already a huge victory.

This movement is winning. It's winning by being broad and inclusive, by emphasizing what we have in common and bridging differences between the homeless, the poor, those in freefall and the fiscally thriving but outraged; between generations, races, and nationalities; and between longtime activists and newcomers. It's winning by keeping its eyes on the prize, which is economic justice and direct democracy, and by living out that direct democracy every day through assemblies and committees.

It's winning through people power and direct-action tactics, from global marches to blockades to many hundreds of occupations. It's winning through the creativity of the young, from the twenty-two-year-old who launched Move Your Money Day to the twenty-six-year-old who started the We Are the 99 Percent website. It's winning through tactics learned from Argentina's 2001 revolution of general assemblies and *política afectiva*, the politics of affection. It's winning by becoming the space in which we are civil society: of human beings in the aggregate, living in public and with trust and love for one another. Violence is not going to be one of the tools that works in this movement.

Violence Is Authoritarian

Bodily violence is a means of coercing others against their will by causing pain, injury, or death. It steals another's bodily integrity or very life as property to dispose of as the violator wishes. Since the majority in our movement would never consent to violent actions, such actions are also imposed on our body politic against our will. This is the very antithesis of anarchy as an ideal in which no one is coerced. If you wish to do something the great majority of us oppose, do it on your own. But these small violent bands attach themselves to large nonviolent movements, perhaps because there aren't any large violent movements around.

As Peter Marshall writes in his history of anarchism, *Demanding the Impossible*, "the word violence comes from the Latin *violare* and etymologically means violation. Strictly speaking, to act violently means to treat others without respect. . . . A violent revolution is therefore unlikely to bring about any fundamental change in human relations . . . Given the anarchists' respect for the sovereignty of the individual, in the long run it is nonviolence and not violence which is implied by anarchist values." Many of us anarchists are not ideological pacifists; I'm more than fine with the ways the Zapatista rebels in southern Mexico have defended themselves and notice how sadly necessary it sometimes is, and I sure wouldn't dictate what Syrians or Tibetans may or may not do. But petty violence in public in this country doesn't achieve anything useful.

Snatching Defeat from the Jaws of Victory

In downtown Oakland, late on the evening of November 2 after a triumphant and mostly nonviolent day of mass actions, a building near Occupy Oakland's encampment was seized, debris was piled up as if to make barricades—show barricades to set afire, not defend—trash cans were set on fire, windows broken, rocks thrown, and then there were altercations with the police. If the goal was to seize a building, one witness pointed out, then seize it secretly, not flamboyantly. The activity around the seizure seemed intended to bait the police into action. Which worked; police are not hard to bait. Activists and police were injured. What was achieved?

Many other activists yelled at the brawlers because they felt that the violence-tinged actions did not represent them or the Occupy movement and put them in danger. It was appalling that the city of Oakland began, a week earlier, by sending in stormtrooper police before dawn rather than negotiating about the fate of the Occupy Oakland encampment. But it was ridiculous that some people tried to get the police to be violent all over again. And it was tragic that others bore the brunt of that foray, including the grievously injured veteran Kayvan Sabeghi—another veteran, a week after Scott Olsen.

Earlier this fall, the publishing group CrimethInc issued a screed in justification of violence that's being circulated widely in the Occupy movement. It's titled "Dear Occupiers: A Letter from Anarchists," though most anarchists I know would disagree with almost everything that follows. Midway through, it declares, "Not everyone is resigned to legalistic pacifism; some people still remember how to stand up for themselves . . . Assuming that those at the front of clashes with the authorities are somehow in league with the authorities is not only illogical . . . This allegation is typical of privileged people who have been taught to trust the authorities and fear everyone who disobeys them."

If nonviolence and people power is privilege, explain this eyewitness account from Oakland last Wednesday, posted on the Occupy Oakland site by Kallista Patridge:

By the time we got to the University building, a brave man was blocking the door screaming "Peaceful Protest! This is my city, and I don't want to destroy it!" He cracked his knuckles, ready to take on an attack, his face splattered in paint from the Whole Foods fiasco [in which downtown Oakland's branch of the chain store was spraypainted and smashed up based on a rumor that workers were told they'd be fired if they took the day off for the General Strike]. Behind the doors were men in badges. I was now watching a black man shield cops from a protest. The black flag group began pointing out those attempting to stop them, chanting "The peace police must be stopped," and I was, personally, rather disgusted by the strategy of comparing peacefully pissed people to police.

The protester who gave this account also noted that in downtown Oakland that day a couple of men with military-style haircuts and brand new clothes put bandanas over their faces and began to smash stuff. She thinks that infiltrators were part of the property destruction and maybe instigated it, and Copwatch's posted video seems to document police infiltrators at Occupy Oakland. One way to be impossible to sabotage is to be clearly committed to tactics that the state can't co-opt. If an infiltrator wants to nonviolently blockade or march or take out the garbage, well, that's one more of us. If an infiltrator sabotages us by recruiting for mayhem, that's a comment on what those tactics are good for.

What Actually Works

The language of CrimethInc is empty machismo peppered with insults, and just in this tiny snippet, incoherent. People who don't like violence are not necessarily fearful or obedient; people power and nonviolence are strategies that are not the same as the ideology of pacifism. To shut down the whole central city of Seattle and the World Trade Organization ministerial meeting on November 30, 1999, or the business district of San Francisco for three days in March of 2003, or the Port

REBECCA SOLNIT

of Oakland on November 2, 2011—all through people power—
is one hell of a great way to stand up. It works. And it brings
great joy and a sense of power to those who do it. It's how the
world gets changed these days.

CrimethInc, whose logo is its name inside a bullet, doesn't
actually cite examples of violence achieving anything in our
recent history. Can you name any? The anonymous writers
don't seem prepared to act, they just tell others to (as do the
two most high-profile advocates of violence on the left). And
despite the smear quoted above that privileged people oppose them, theirs is the language of privilege. White kids can
do crazy shit and get slapped on the wrist or maybe slapped
around for it; I have for a quarter century walked through police lines like they were tall grass; people of color face far more
dire consequences. When white youth try to bring the police
down on a racially diverse movement—well, it's not exactly
what the word "solidarity" means to most of us.

Another Occupy Oakland witness, a female street medic,
wrote of the ill-conceived late-night antics of November 2:
"watching Black Bloc-ers run from the cops and not protect
the camp their actions had endangered, an action which ultimately left behind many mentally ill people, sick people,
street kids, and homeless folks to defend themselves against
the police onslaught, was disturbing and disgusting in ways I
can't even articulate because I am still so angry at the empty
bravado and cowardice that I saw." She adds: "I want those
kids to be held accountable to the damage that they did, damage made possible by their class and race privilege." And
physical fitness—Occupy Oakland's camp includes children,
older people, wheelchair users and a lot of other people less
ready to run.

How We Defeated the Police

The euphemism for violence is "diversity of tactics," perhaps
because diversity has been a liberal-progressive buzzword
these past decades. But diversity does not mean that anything

goes and that democratic decision-making doesn't apply. If you want to be part of a movement, treat the others with respect; don't spring unwanted surprises on them—particularly surprises that sabotage their own tactics—and chase away the real diversity of the movement. Most of us don't want to be part of an action that includes those tactics. If you want to fight the police, look at who's succeeded in changing their behavior: lawyers, lawmakers, police watchdog groups like Copwatch, investigative journalists (including a friend of mine whose work just put several New Orleans policemen in prison for decades), neighborhood patrols, community organizers, grassroots movements, often two or more players working together. You have to build.

The night after the raid on Oakland, the police were massed to raid Occupy San Francisco. About two thousand of us stood in and around the Occupy encampment as helicopters hovered. Nonviolence trainers helped people prepare to blockade. Because we had a little political revolt against the Democratic money machine ten years ago and began to elect progressives who actually represent us pretty well, five of our city supervisors, the public defender, and a state senator—all people of color, incidentally—stood with us all night, vowing they would not let this happen.

We stood up. We fought a nonviolent battle against four hundred riot police that was so effective the police didn't even dare show up. That's people power. The same day Occupy Oakland took its campsite back, with people power, and the Black Bloc kids were reportedly part of the whole: they dismantled the cyclone fencing panels and stacked them up neatly. That's how Occupy San Francisco won. And that's how Occupy Oakland won.

State troopers and city police refused to break up the Occupy Albany encampment in New York state, despite the governor's and mayor's orders. Sometimes the police can be swayed. Not by violence, though. The master's tools won't dismantle the master's house. And they sure won't build a better house.

People Power Shapes the World

Left violence failed miserably in the 1970s: the squalid and futile violence in Germany and Italy; the delusional Symbionese Liberation Army murdering Marcus Foster, Oakland's first black school superintendent, and later gunning down a bystander mother of four in a bank; the bumbling Weather Underground accidentally blowing three of its members up and turning the rest into fugitives for a decade; all of them giving us a bad name we've worked hard to escape.

Think of that excruciating footage in Sam Green's *Weather Underground* documentary of the "days of rage," when a handful of delusions-of-grandeur young white radicals thought they'd do literal battle with the Chicago police and thus inspire the working class to rise up. The police clobbered them; the working class was so not impressed. If you want to address a larger issue, getting overly entangled with local police is a great way to lose focus and support.

In fact, the powerful and effective movements of the past sixty years have been almost entirely nonviolent. The civil rights movement included the Deacons for Defense, but the focus of that smaller group was actually defense—the prevention of violence against nonviolent activists and the movement, not offensive forays. Jonathan Schell points out that even the French and Russian Revolutions were largely nonviolent when it came to overthrowing the old regime; seizing a monopoly of power to form a new regime is when the blood really began to flow.

I think of the Sandinista Revolution of 1979 as the last great armed revolution, and it succeeded because the guerrillas with guns who came down from the mountains had wide popular support. People power. People power overthrew the Shah of Iran that year, in a revolution that was hijacked by authoritarians fond of violence. In 1986, the Marcos regime of the Philippines was overthrown by nonviolent means, means so compelling the army switched sides and refused to support the Marcos regime.

Armies generally don't do that if you shoot at them (and if you really defeated the police in battle—all the police, nationwide—you'd face the army). Since then dozens of regimes, from South Africa, Hungary, Czechoslovakia, Poland, and Nepal, to Bolivia, Argentina, Uruguay, Brazil, and Tunisia, have been profoundly changed through largely nonviolent means. There was self-defense in the Deacons for Defense style in the Egyptian uprising this year, but people power was the grand strategy that brought out the millions and changed the country. Armed struggle was part of the ongoing resistance in South Africa, but in the end people power and international solidarity were the fulcra of change. The Zapatistas used violence sparingly as a last resort, but "Our word is our weapon," they say, and they used other tools in preference, often and exquisitely.

The powerful and effective movements of the past sixty years have used the strategy of people power. It works. It changes the world. It's changing the world now. Join us. Or don't join us. But please don't try to have it both ways.

Joanna Neborsky

SCENES FROM OCCUPIED PHILADEL- PHIA

NIKIL SAVAL

October 27

What coalesced slowly and warily in New York sprung up in Philadelphia overnight. Massive tents; a welter of information tables near the Dilworth Plaza subway entrance; a permit from the city. The encampment, directly across the street from city hall, is shaggy but impressive. "This is real," reads one poster. The first night, around one AM, Mayor Michael Nutter emerges from City Hall to do a meet-and-greet with the occupiers, declaring that he, too, is part of the 99 percent—which, technically speaking, must be true.

I walk around Philadelpia during the day extremely conscious of there being a tent city in the very center of town. When I walk to the plaza to attend a GA, or simply for a whirl through—it has become obligatory, when friends come to town, to "go see the occupation"—I pass hundreds of people who surprise me in having other things to do. It astonishes me that there is anything else to do besides goggle at the extraordinary collective serving food to the homeless, drumming, and doing yoga in full view of the city government, day after day after day. I sometimes start to feel the same way about myself, wondering what I'm doing not occupying: going to a movie instead of GA, cooking dinner instead of GA, sitting at my computer instead of GA.

Every GA I do attend seems to take two to three hours, during which people drift in and out, some of them shouting obscenities and clearly in need of medical help. At one of them, the legal group explains that the city has offered to meet with the occupiers on a weekly basis. Legal proposes that a core negotiating committee be formed, comprised of two to three members from each working group on a rotating basis—a proposal so sound I can barely stand it. But a sizable portion of the GA sniffs vanguardism and proposes instead that the city come down to GA—an amendment so insane that I begin to doubt the capacity of my fellow assemblymen and women to govern themselves. In the end the proposal is delayed for a later meeting.

NIKIL SAVAL

After a time, the occupation starts to seem—like the city hall which shades it—stately and inert. The politics become subservient to the proliferating logistics necessary to maintain the encampment. There are actions and marches, none of them exceptionally large. At around noon on a blustery day under a tin-colored sky, I attend a scraggly labor rally, sidling along with the young staff of UNITE HERE, the union I do volunteer research for. A representative from the Philadelphia AFL-CIO chapter—an almost prototypical union hand, doughy, his slate-gray hair slicked back—tells us to fight for the Prez's jobs plan. Very few people from the occupation march with us. At lunchtime, the line of homeless holding plates and utensils snakes out from the kitchen.

I read of camps being evicted in Atlanta and Oakland the same night that I get an urgent and lucid email, sent out to various working groups of the Philadelphia occupation, detailing the medical and sanitation crisis afflicting the encampment, due to the influx of homeless people in need of real services. Fights have broken out; someone was caught doing crack in their tent—a fact less alarming because of the drug and more because of the presence of fire among highly flammable tents. "Our homeless population is in need of services and care," wrote the author of the email, a longtime community organizer and activist, "but service providers funded through the city have balked at the idea of appearing to support an Occupation for fear of being defunded." Therefore they are not coming into the camp, and the crisis grows. The organizer proposes "a dual-site restructuring of the encampment," separating the aspects devoted to just camping out—sanitation, food, medical—and the political goals.

It strikes me at once as the most intelligent idea I've heard, and a useful concession to the idea that the occupations cannot model the society they want to see in the world from day one. In fact, they expose everything our society fails to provide, neglects to care about. At the same time there is something cruel about the proposal: It is sane and reasonable, but it is also suggesting we need to cut ourselves off from the homeless in order to survive. I don't know what to think.

I miss the GA where the proposal is aired, but I learn later that the sanitation and medical crisis resolves itself organically. The sanitation crew works overtime; the medical tent also. The camp soldiers on, the same.

November 11

It is the largest GA I've seen since the first days. A line of poetry comes to me: "Vaster than empires, and more slow." It follows a week of GAs devoted entirely to discussing the proposal which comes up for a vote today: whether to expand the encampment across the street to Thomas Paine Plaza. The city has been warning that it has had longstanding plans to begin a renovation project in Dilworth Plaza, to make the subway handicap accessible and to build a reflecting pool that would double as an ice-skating rink in the winter. Informal conversation with building trades union members suggests that the project isn't shovel-ready: there are no signed contracts, only plans. Still, expressing a willingness to move would imply an openness to the movement, a sense of clarity over the real target—inequality, financialization, a broken political system—and proof that it's about the 99 percent, not a piece of pavement.

The first night of discussion, a week ago, was led by the "radical caucus," a strange group of pretty stern-looking folks, dressed in all black. One of their most vocal members had a Stalin mustache, which harmonized uneasily with his soul patch. When asked by the facilitator to read their proposal, one of the members responded: "We propose to resist eviction." The facilitator asked if there was any more to the proposal. There wasn't. Concerns and clarifying questions were frequently met with exaggeratedly disbelieving and baffled expressions from the radical caucus; occasionally, Stalin moustache would visibly mouth, "What the fuck is she talking about?" "Solidarity with Oakland" was one of the reasons for

NIKIL SAVAL

staying; another was not wanting to be seen as caving to the authorities. A number of people made the reasonable point that blocking this particular development was not the issue; another suggested that, furthermore, blocking the development would prevent access for the disabled to the subway. It went on like this for over three hours in the cold. The radical caucus's proposal was tabled, to be discussed again later.

Today, the lingering frustration of these endless debates saps my willingness to endure them yet again. I'm only two hours in and I leave in frustration, after I hear someone compare this struggle to King making his stand at Selma. The occupations have provoked an epidemic of this kind of political grandiosity. It feels like the retromania of pop music critics, who can't review a new artist without comparing him to Dylan or the Boss. I also feel that I don't have a right to vote on where the occupiers stay, as much as I am invited to. Finally I am confident that the vote will go well, that reason will prevail, having heard as much from discussions with participants at GAs past.

I catch a late showing of the new Lars von Trier film, *Melancholia*. People at a country estate watch as a rogue planet, hidden behind the sun until now, speeds along on a collision course with the earth—all to the tune of the Prelude to *Tristan und Isolde*. In the final minutes, Charlotte Gainsbourg suggests that they all have a glass of wine out on the verandah, as a sort of final act. Kirsten Dunst does not want to, however. "You know what I think of your plan?" Kirsten Dunst says. "I think it's a piece of shit."

I arrive home, invigorated by nihilism, and discover that, after five hours of discussion—by which point many of the people gathered had left—the GA has voted to stay in Dilworth Plaza! The city is not happy. The labor working group email list is not happy. There were enough trigger-happy people to make this fateful decision, and I can't even imagine they're happy. "Una festa amara," is the headline on one of the Italian newspapers, describing the rally in Rome that followed Berlusconi's resignation: a bitter celebration. I pour myself a beer and pray for the destruction of the planet. I realize that I should have stayed and fought, even if my vote or my "clarifying questions" wouldn't have saved the day. I had a responsibility to do so. I suppose I hadn't realized how much I cared.

The next morning, I read more emails: social movements suffer setbacks, they make decisions that they can reverse, this isn't the only time a potential move will be debated, etc. It's true, and it makes me think that a disaffection with the importance of holding a single space will move outward— "horizontally," as an occupier would say—to the rest of the 99 percent. Perhaps there will be general assemblies in the future that are less about how to live, more about what to do. The decision may have woken everyone up from the self-love that had come to afflict our bitter celebration; after all, the point was never just to hold a park.

NIKIL SAVAL

THE HOMELESS QUESTION

CHRISTOPHER HERRING & ZOLTÁN GLÜCK

We were sitting on the raised flowerbed along the southern perimeter of Liberty Plaza, chatting while we finished our meals. The din of the General Assembly meeting could be heard in the background and Harris was telling me about the punk band he'd been in during the '80s when three men came over and interrupted. "This is the guy I was telling you about, who the police told to come here." Bob, an old-timer I've seen around at a number of marches and OWS events, had been talking with us earlier about being homeless in New York. Now he was back with these two men, one of them apparently from "legal." They were eager to hear Harris's story about how he'd been sleeping uptown, in the same place he'd been sleeping for years, when two police officers woke him up, told him that there had been a complaint, and suggested that he "go down to Zuccotti."

Harris talked about how he knew everyone in the neighborhood and has never caused any trouble, and how it seemed impossible that someone would all of a sudden raise a complaint. The man from legal then interjected: "So, then it's confirmed. The police are actually doing this." There was a pause and then he looked directly at Harris and said sternly: "Go back uptown."

It took a moment to register that this was an act of banishment. The silence was broken by Bob, supplicating awkwardly, "But wait, no, Harris is actually a good guy. Like I was saying…" Harris was quick with a response that dissolved the tension. "I'm not sleeping here." He had been distributing chocolate throughout the day, he said. "The problem with these other homeless people who are coming down here is that they are not contributing."

The conversation now turned to why "contributing" should be the basic criteria for whether the homeless are allowed to stay. The legal attaché waxed political about how freeloaders were bad for the movement, but that homeless who are willing to contribute could be an asset. Then the two men asked Harris if he would make a proposal to the General Assembly summing up their conversation. Harris declined, but they

CHRISTOPHER HERRING & ZOLTÁN GLÜCK

persuaded him to dictate a message that they could read on his behalf. I was appointed scribe and wrote down his declaration:

If you are not contributing to the movement, then why are you here? If you do not go on marches, why are you here? This is a society of people who have come together to protest. If you are not protesting, why are you here? This is not a place for free food or free cigarettes. If you live in New York, go home. If you are homeless in New York, there are plenty of places to be homeless. Go there. Feel free to visit, maybe even eat some free food, occasionally. But don't stay here. Don't cause trouble. This society gives us enough trouble.

Encounters and conversations like this have been playing out at occupations across the United States. Based on our observations, the general exclusion of the homeless from public life has already begun to take root in the Occupy movement. The political calculus of whether the homeless "deserve" to be a part of the movement threatens to reproduce existing forms of structural violence and exclusion within the heart of the movement.

An Asset or a Risk?

On one side of the equation, the homeless have been portrayed as instrumental allies: bringing numbers to the cause, helping to hold down sparser occupations as winter hardens, sharing tactics about sleeping rough, and proving powerful symbols of the economic system's brutality. More frequently, though, the homeless have been portrayed as a detriment and a risk: diverting energy away from fighting the real issues, exacerbating the problems of cleanliness within the camp, offending the sensibilities of middle-class campers, verbally or physically assaulting passersby and participants, and polluting the image of an orderly protest. These negative representations of a nefarious underclass co-opting the occupations have made it easier for Occupy's opponents to belittle the movement as vagrant and lawless, putting pressure on municipal authorities to crack down. Indeed, the largest risk seems to lie in this politics of representation, through which municipal governments might convert the question of occupation from a political right of protest to a question of "public health and safety"—the classic premise used against homeless encampments for decades.

Through these representations of the homeless, both in the media and at times within the movement itself, the homeless question has become framed as an informal calculus of the costs and benefits of including or excluding the most brutally impoverished. At this critical moment in the progress of the movement, the homeless question has become a question of exclusion, legitimacy, and belonging.

There is a series of problems involved in conflating the right to camp with a responsibility to contribute. First, the question of "contribution" and demanding proof of support for the cause is discriminatory; it is a burden faced only by those who "appear homeless." Those who can pass for "real protesters" in their dress, disposition, and discussion are considered assets in their mere presence and rarely questioned. Second, it is important to remember that many of the Occupy camps have co-opted public spaces that had long been occupied by the homeless, and in some cases have even displaced these populations. In some cases, the protests have even inadvertently drawn violence toward these rough sleepers. One homeless woman we spoke to in Oakland, who had been sleeping around Oscar Grant Plaza long before the occupation, complained of being tear-gassed and robbed in the wake of a protest. Third, the dichotomy of "contributing" and "freeloading" mirrors the more general divisive distinctions between the deserving and undeserving poor.

We must therefore reframe the homeless question beyond the division between those "dissenting" and those "seeking shelter" (as a *New York Times* headline had it). Although some homeless people may be converted to the goals of dissent,

CHRISTOPHER HERRING & ZOLTÁN GLÜCK

many will not or cannot, and the movement must take special care not to instrumentalize this precarious group. At the same time, opposing the survival goals of the homeless and the political goals of the occupiers has led to discriminatory practices at OWS and elsewhere, such as those of the Zuccotti kitchen staff who were recently embroiled in accusations of discrimination against those who appeared to be "professionally homeless."

The "homeless problem" of OWS is not a problem of the movement, but rather of the economic system at which it is aimed. It is a problem that society ignores or treats through punishment and exclusion, but the movement cannot afford to respond to it in this way. The "homeless question" should be reframed as a question of how dissenters should treat those seeking food and a safe place to sleep. Rather than supporting a politics of exclusion toward the homeless, some occupations have explicitly taken up their cause. The kitchens at Occupy Oakland and Occupy Philadelphia openly aim to feed the city's homeless. In Atlanta, protesters are working to save a shelter that is at risk of shutting down, and in Austin the movement has mobilized to push for more affordable housing and to legalize tent cities for the homeless. These efforts point to what new forms of solidarity and alliance could look like. Although protesters and the homeless may differ in their use of occupied spaces, the movement cannot afford to let this difference mask the more relevant question of why both groups have come to share the same ground.

"Why Are You Here?"

The way Harris used the rhetorical question "Why are you here?" to shame the "undeserving" resonates with the homeless question currently posed both in the media and within parts of the movement itself. It is important for the movement to take Harris's question seriously and to articulate why it is that scores of homeless have flocked to occupations for relief. Why are the homeless at these occupations rather than other public places? In our discussions with the homeless in New York and Oakland, it became apparent that they are simultaneously being pushed by the state, directed to the park by the police, and pulled in by the failure of miserly welfare policies, preferring to eat in an environment without the demeaning rituals of shelters and soup kitchens.

Jane, an African-American woman in her forties who has only recently become homeless, was staying at a shelter in Richmond until Occupy Oakland set up camp in Frank Ogawa Plaza. Although she complains about the colder weather, she prefers her outdoor campsite to the shelter bed. "That shelter is dangerous, dirty, and the staff treats you like shit. Here, I feel like I have a voice, and people treat you like a real person. I can weather this cold for a bit of dignity." Jim, a homeless man who has lived on the streets for over a decade and is sympathetic but not contributing to the movement, has been spending more and more time around Oakland's encampment. "Cops and businesses give you a hard time around this city, telling you to move on. It's nice to have a space where you don't feel threatened."

In this respect, many occupations are incubating a movement to address the punitive practices of banishment against the chronically homeless. These practices are also inherent in what's left of our degrading welfare provisions, which observe—with parsimonious strictness—distinctions between the "deserving" and "undeserving" poor. At the same time, those in the movement are understandably concerned that such a strategy might overwhelm the camps' capacities and, in becoming the primary function of the site, obfuscate a cause whose goals are much broader.

As we move forward, grappling with both immediate and long-term questions about the place of the homeless in this movement, it is essential that we remember the systemic and historical connections that bind us together. That the history of capitalism is also the history of systemic social and economic exclusion. And that today we are all at risk of becoming part of the *relative surplus population*.

CHRISTOPHER HERRING & ZOLTÁN GLÜCK

Moments of expulsion and economic relegation have occurred in fits and spurts throughout modern history, but they
are most acute during periods of general economic crisis. It is
therefore to this logic of exclusion and crisis that we should
look to in posing the question "Why are you here?" What is
important is that the answer actually encompasses both the
homeless and the broader OWS movement—both have been
brought into existence by economic marginalization, crisis,
and expulsion. We must understand that a common logic
underlies the mass foreclosures, the expulsion of low- and
middle-income earners from their homes, the emergence of
an indebted and seemingly economically redundant generation of students, the growth of mass incarceration as a tool for
containing impoverished populations, the widespread and
growing homelessness of the past forty years, and the racial
dynamics that play out in these processes. It is no simple coincidence that street homelessness reemerged in America at
the same historical moment that the top one percent began
its rapid ascent, in the early 1970s. It is only when we take
our common predicament seriously that we can answer the
question of why we are here. We each have our own story,
but ultimately we have arrived together at this juncture of
precariousness, insecurity, and exclusion. This common predicament must become a source of solidarity and a foundation
for the difficult task of building a new politics of inclusion.

SCENES FROM OCCUPIED BOSTON

STEPHEN SQUIBB

October 6

When I first arrived at Dewey Square in Boston, I could not find the occupation. It was blocked by a farmer's market. I had grown up half an hour west of here, in Wayland, but I was disoriented: This space used to be the expressway, a raised portion of I-93 running through the heart of Boston, past the North End, Boston Garden, and down to Logan Airport. The Big Dig had buried it, yielding a small park, a farmer's market, and then, as I discovered walking further north, an impressive procession of tents spilling out behind the merchants selling artisanal breads and local cheese. Many were covered by shiny blue tarps.

The cars whizzed by along Atlantic Avenue, past South Station, most of them heading for the entrance to the Mass Pike. They saw several dozen people holding signs with various slogans; one half honked in solidarity, the other half yelled, "Get a job!"

I finally presented myself at the media tent, invited by a large yellow sign, hastily scrawled in red marker: "VOLUNTEERS needed, got five minutes or five hours?"

"I can volunteer," I told Adrienne, seated behind the table. She offered to train me on media and twenty minutes later I was burrowed in a pile of email, trying to connect disparate points of information. People would show up and ask about getting involved with outreach, with music or art projects, or people knew someone who wanted to give a lecture. The work often involved creating organization on the fly. At that point, most communications came through one account, commboston@gmail.com, which many of us had access to. In fact, I had been given access within ten minutes of arriving.

Over the next several days that one account would split into dozens, as working groups began setting up accounts of their own. I spent that time both searching for hierarchy and living in fear of being discovered. Every time a new person walked into the tent, I thought: At last, this is the person in charge. They will now ask me who I am, and what I am doing here, and I don't know what I will say. But this never happened.

October 10

The GA had renamed today "Indigenous People's Day," and the scheduled solidarity march between students and unions was expecting good turnout. It had been decided that under cover of the march, or in honor of it, we would expand camp across the street, farther down the Greenway. We needed more room.

There was concern that the expansion would immediately trigger a raid by the police. This necessitated moving communications offsite so that we could continue texting and tweeting and livestreaming if the police came into the camp. The plan was two-fold: first, to run communications from a nearby office during the march; and, two, to have press releases ready for different scenarios so that we could respond immediately. We had one for no arrests; one for some arrests; and one for a complete takedown. We had stayed up late sending drafts back and forth.

We couldn't get to the off-site office until after the march started, as the person with access to it was working. Angie and I ran messages between the marchers and camp, and tweeted information and requests from a Starbucks as the first wave of students passed by us. Both of us dashed out to stand and cheer before going back in to estimate numbers and the time the students would meet the column of workers advancing from the north. The plan was for the students to converge with the workers, including ironworkers from Local 7, and march to the North Washington Bridge. The bridge was in need of serious repair; the ironworkers happened to be in serious need of work.

Eventually we got to our office, and my colleagues agreed to let me go to the march. The march was a magnificent thing, many thousands strong. The weather was fine, and Direct Action did expert work with the route and pacing. When we arrived at the bridge we found that the police had formed a line of motorcycles blocking us from approaching. An initial surge left one protester in cuffs as the march crashed and receded. One young man, white, tall, with a beard, shouted, "Take the bridge!"

"Brother!" broke in a short black woman of about forty in a MASS UNITING t-shirt. "Brother, across that bridge, that's Eastie! You don't want to go there!"

An impromptu GA sprung up, debating whether to take the bridge (and potentially enter East Boston), stay in solidarity with the arrested protester, or return to camp. The members of the Direct Action group, who were in all black, joined hands, creating a black snake through the crowd. Over by the edge, where the crowd began to thin out, we knelt down in the middle of the road. Traffic had been stopped but we could see up the street that four large wagons were waiting in the event of arrests. Three members of the group unfurled black flags above our heads and a discussion began that mirrored the one going on in the larger group: What were we going to do?

While we were discussing, I got a text: "Expansion complete." The other camp had been taken. I relayed this to our discussion group and we decided to return home to defend camp. B., black mask hanging at her neck, grinned as she announced consensus, her ten fingers wiggling up toward the clear October sky.

Back at the camp, word was police were giving us until midnight to clear the new encampment. It was unknown if they were going to clear the old one too, while they were at it. We headed back to the office, where we had left our gear, to put out the call for reinforcements, tweeting things like, "Which side are you on, Boston? History wants to know." And "Come write your grandkid's favorite story." We asked people to call the various authorities and demand that we be allowed to stay. I don't know where we got the idea for the hotel, but it came up somehow; the office was comfortable, but we couldn't see the camp from it, whereas the luxury Intercontinental Hotel likely had rooms looking out over the expansion. When we arrived at the front desk, I identified myself as a journalist in need of a room overlooking the park. The first room they gave us didn't have the right view, so Angie immediately demanded another, while I messed with the press releases.

The new camp was on a new patch of park, and as the evening wore on about a thousand people gathered in response to our pleas. A lot of these were photographers and videographers whose presence we had requested especially. The police, in the meantime, had begun distributing leaflets that declared their intention to videotape the proceedings to better identify and prosecute those engaged in "criminal disorder" after the fact. Everybody was telling everybody they were going to be watching. At midnight, the first ambulances started to show up, parked in a row on the far side of the park.

October 11

The police had told the media to leave, as their safety could no longer be assured. Several stayed anyway, along with our own photographers and videographers. We watched as the streets were slowly shut down, and lines of police marched in to barricade the park, including a special line of transit police, dressed in black and armed with long, flexible white batons. They looked like ultraviolent mimes. Meanwhile, a ring of protesters, arms locked, had formed around the tents, while the Veterans for Peace marched in circles, their white flags flapping in the wind. They formed a line between the transit police and the camp. Several hundred protesters who did not want to be arrested were gathered at the southeast corner. What happened next has been well documented. The police moved in, knocking the veterans to the ground, and began clearing the protesters and tearing down the camp. They destroyed the entirety of the extension but left the original occupation untouched, arresting 141 people. We knew they were coming, we were prepared, and nobody was seriously hurt. Yet, even knowing that, it is a difficult experience to describe. Watching from the twelfth floor as the state assembled and then deployed its forces against our friends seemed to rupture something, as though every previous experience of anxiety or dread had been subject to a secret limit that had suddenly been removed.

Afterwards, we packed up and vacated one by one, until only three of us remained. I went downstairs to get Nadir, a squash coach and fearless occupier who had come to retrieve the video editing gear he had stashed in our room. When I got to the lobby I could see him speaking with the police outside. Somebody who appeared to be either a manager or an undercover cop approached me. He told me we were being asked to leave. I asked for a couple of hours to clean up. He could give us five minutes. When it took longer than that, four police officers showed up at our room and urged us out as quickly as possible.

I slept for three hours and awoke to a collective inbox overflowing with media requests. We assigned as many as we could. I lost track of the radio interviews. I remember a phone call with a *Globe* editorial writer as I walked through my campus. Had the movement been taken over by anarchists?

I was affronted. "THE ASSERTION THAT THE MOVEMENT HAS BEEN TAKEN OVER BY RADICALS IS LUDICROUS."

"Uh huh," he said.

"THE CHARGE OF ANARCHISM HAS ALWAYS BEEN A FILTHY SMEAR ON THE LIPS OF THE RULING CLASS."

His editorial was actually pretty sympathetic. But, I mean, it was like asking if the South Pole had been "taken over" by penguins; the occupation has been anarchist from the start. Later we were contacted by *Countdown with Keith Olbermann*; they wanted to talk with the people who ran the livestream. My last memory of the day was sitting in a closet studio in downtown Boston, not nearly as large as the media tent. They put my earpiece in; I jotted a few notes, and, waiting to go live, I felt alone for the first time in days. I spent seven or so minutes speaking with the disembodied voice of Keith Olbermann while they ran our footage. I stopped by camp to check on people getting bailed out, and then went home and fell asleep.

RUMORS

ASTRA TAYLOR & SARAH RESNICK

If an American was condemned to confine his activity to his own affairs, he would be robbed of one half of his existence; he would feel an immense void in the life which he is accustomed to lead, and his wretchedness would be unbearable.
—Alexis de Tocqueville, 1835

Monday, October 17

Astra:

Right before midnight I tuned into the Zuccotti Park livestream. I had been down there earlier that afternoon, but I still felt compelled to check in. Though the encampment, with the help of a couple thousand early-rising allies, had successfully resisted city's eviction attempt days before, I had a lingering sense that the occupation was something precious that may dissipate or be destroyed as quickly as it had emerged, as if from nowhere. Indeed, when the video finally buffered and began to play, it looked as though my concerns were about to be validated. I couldn't quite discern what was happening the image was dark and blurry, the audio disjointed—but the police were definitely moving in. They were angry about a tent, and a confrontation was brewing. Tents had been a point of contention since the beginning of the occupation, with any semblance of a semi-permanent structure serving as a pretext for officers to march into the park, tear it down, and arrest a few people in the process. "The constitution doesn't protect tents," Mayor Bloomberg declared. "It protects speech and assembly."

While protesters seemed to be reconciled to camping out wrapped in blankets and tarps, the medical tent was different. Someone told me that the National Nurses United, already providing training and support to demonstrators at occupations across the country, had petitioned Bloomberg to make an exception for the sake of public health. A tent was erected to serve this purpose. I braced myself for a fight as I watched a human chain form around its periphery, sick at the prospect of watching people get clobbered in real-time. But it didn't happen. Instead, unannounced and unexpected, his timing impeccable, Jesse Jackson waltzed into the park and seamlessly linked arms with the demonstrators to defend against the dismantling. "Jesse Jackson!" people screamed, and the scene suddenly shifted from anxious to exuberant. Faced with a celebrity-endorsed blockade, the police backed down, and in the ensuing days I noticed more and more tents popping up.

On Fri, Oct 21, 2011 at 3:23 PM, Astra Taylor wrote:

Sarah, I just got this forwarded by a friend. Should we investigate? I want to know what the hell is going on. The idea that the encampment may implode over drumming would be laughable if it weren't so depressing, and an actual possibility. So many movements and groups have destroyed themselves from the inside out. Will this happen to OWS too? I hope not.

"X says a woman who's been very disruptive . . . managed to get folks on board with the idea that the oppression of the drummers is a civil rights issue. She's rallying POC folks to meet at 5:45 at the red tripod sculpture with the drummers, to march from there to the community board meeting playing drums as loudly as they can."

Friday, October 21

Sarah R:

A group of rogue drummers planned to march to a meeting with Community Board One to let them hear what they thought of the "Good Neighbor Policy." Posted throughout the park, the policy asked that (among other things) drumming be limited to two hours a day so the neighbors—not to mention the demonstrators—could have some quiet. Yet for the drummers, two hours would not suffice—it was a quelling of free expression. And as of earlier that week, various listservs and social media were sounding the alarm: Our

ASTRA TAYLOR & SARAH RESNICK

under-recognized allies at the community board had grown
tired of the endless reverberations against the glass and steel
of the neighborhood buildings. Until now, we were told, they
had supported the occupation, and their endorsement was
not without its rewards. We could thank them, for instance,
for their part in thwarting the plans for "cleaning" the park.
It's true, apparently. At a wedding, a state senator—who had
played middleman between the community board, the park
owners, and the protesters—proudly displayed his text messages with some higher-up at Brookfield to a friend. But that
was last week, and now, apparently, the neighbors were mad.
The community board was losing patience and support was
waning. And if they turned against the movement, another
eviction attempt would surely follow. Or so we'd heard.

So I met up with Astra at the park at 5:30 PM and we lingered by the di Suvero sculpture. We were curious; concerned,
too. And we wanted to see what would happen. But no group
amassed. And over on the west end of the park, there was no
indication the drums would ever let up. We grew sure that
our lead was a non event. And we were pleased! Perhaps the
community meeting would end well after all. And we found
out later it did—better, at least, than expected. The neighbors
voted to give OWS another chance, though they implored the
drumming be curtailed.

On the train platform, we discussed second occupation
attempts—past failures, future possibilities. Rumors. We
deliberated over strategy and contemplated symbolic res-
onance. We put forth suggestions—places we'd like to see
taken—though they were reveries to be sure. I prattled on
until I realized Astra was no longer listening. She had turned
toward a short, forty-something woman in a navy suit and
loafer flats who stood not three feet away. The woman stared
right past us, still and unblinking. And it was clear that she
was trying to look natural, ordinary, casual. But she was holding up her cell phone in the least natural way, her elbow bent,
her forearm straight up—gravity wouldn't like it that way.
She's filming us, we said.

The woman stepped forward; she was at a different angle now. And her arm was still up! Astra, much taller than her, maybe even by a whole foot, bent down and leaned in close. Are you filming us? Is your camera on? I peered at the ID card on a lanyard around her neck. She works at Deloitte. But her eyes stayed straight out in front, and if she saw or heard us (and she must have!) there was no sign of recognition, no reflex response. And her arm was still up and her phone was pointed toward us. The train finally came and we walked down the platform, bewildered and laughing. In jest, we foretold of the FBI admiring our sweet faces in no less than an hour. Though without saying so we knew there were things less likely. She'd mistaken us for figures of import, radicals of influence, though we knew we were not.

I moved to the back window, hoping to catch a glimpse of her in the next car. Maybe she's just one of those people who films everything, I mused. Like that artist Wafaa Bilal. Unlikely, we both agreed. If our spy was in the adjacent car, she was out of sight.

The doors opened at the next station. "Slavoj!" Astra called through the rush-hour crowd. And Žižek maneuvered his way to where we were standing. We recounted our tale of citizen surveillance, and he complained of the hippies at Occupy San Francisco. At Union Square, we exited the train and he called out after Astra: "I hear you are married. Don't you know that's a sin!"

ASTRA TAYLOR & SARAH RESNICK

Sunday, October 23

Astra:

Back at Zuccotti, this time to meet Judith Butler, who has agreed to give a short speech, an "open forum," as these events are called. A few dozen people gather around her, sitting on steps and crouched on concrete. "It matters that as bodies we arrive together in public, that we are assembling in public; we are coming together as bodies in alliance in the street and in the square," she says, every few words repeated by the human microphone—our bodies, our voices, her amplification. "As bodies we suffer, we require shelter and food, and as bodies we require one another and desire one another. So this is a politics of the public body, the requirements of the body, its movement and voice."

Tuesday, October 25

Astra:

Today I went to Penn Station to pick up my sister Tara, visiting from Georgia. We went straight to Zuccotti Park, arriving around 8:30 PM to watch the General Assembly. A woman, who looked to be in her early thirties, was submitting a proposal to buy fifteen walkie-talkies to be used by the people who watch over the occupation at night. She was requesting $800. She explained that there had been some bad stuff going on when people were asleep and the community watch group needed to be able to communicate to keep things safe for everyone. "Like what kind of bad stuff?" a skeptical guy asked. The women replied that there had been reports of fights, drug dealing, theft, and, finally, sexual harassment. Over the last few days I had heard from friends, in person or over email, that security was a growing concern; here it was being publicly discussed. The crowd, however, seemed reluctant to believe these were serious issues until a young fellow from sanitation stepped forward. "We see these things when we clean up," he said. "It's happening. We need to deal with it." After a few clarifying questions—How will the walkie-talkies be charged? Would they accept a smaller number of walkie-talkies? What brand do they plan to purchase?—the proposal finally passed, my sister and I enthusiastically casting a vote to approve the budget. As we strolled around the park, admiring the bicycle-powered generator in the kitchen, the ever-expanding library, the media team, heads bowed over their computers hard at work, it was hard to imagine feeling unsafe. It was getting late and the park was not well lit, but it was full of people and buzzing with energy.

When we returned to my apartment a couple hours later a message from our other sister, Sunaura, awaited us. She had been occupying Oakland and was supposed to be heading to the airport to catch a red eye and join us for a family visit. But instead she and her partner were caught up in protest, a large spontaneous march against the raid on Occupy Oakland the day before. The community, outraged, was fighting back. "I don't know if you can hear me," Sunaura shouted, exultantly, into her phone. "This is amazing! We want to stay! Can you see if you can change our tickets?" Tara and I went online and found our way to a livestream, expecting some rousing spectacle, but what we saw looked disturbingly like a war zone. We found footage of Oakland police shooting tear-gas canisters into the crowd and read reports of rubber bullets being used against demonstrators. Multiple people emailed me a photo of a woman in a wheelchair trapped in a haze of mace, and I started to panic. After a moment of calm reflection, though, we realized it wasn't our sister—Sunaura wouldn't wear that hat. But she still wasn't picking up her phone. Half an hour later we finally got a text. She and her partner got out just as the cops were closing in and would make their flight. The woman from the photo, I learn the next day, is her friend, a talented dancer and dedicated civil disobedient with a long arrest record.

Wednesday, October 26

Sarah R:

A. had texted: "meet 8:30 or 8:45." And I didn't have to ask—he meant the Police Brutality Solidarity march with Oakland. I was already at the GA, and we were debating $20,000 for bail plus one hundred tents plus shipping. We've got plenty in the bank, can't we spare some for Oakland? Yes.

It's almost 9 PM now and I see A. and C. and we hasten down the sidewalk; we're already lagging. We catch up on Church Street, but A. sprints to the front of the march and I don't see him again that night. Later I hear that he and some others had

ASTRA TAYLOR & SARAH RESNICK

stolen orange netting and run through Tribeca, up Church Street and Sixth Avenue, straight onto the set of *Gossip Girl* on MacDougal Street.

But I'm still with C. and we're headed up Broadway. At Prince Street we veer left. To Washington Square! Then we hear it's surrounded, so we swing right onto Mercer Street. More arrests now but we press on, returning to Broadway and up toward Union Square. We've taken the street now and we're walking through traffic. A couple exits their cab to join us. New York is Oakland. Oakland is New York.

Sunday, October 30

Sarah R:

It's more and more difficult to spend time at the park. Turns out, the revolution is but a series of meetings held at far-flung locations, and I sat in on three today. Four if you count the one in the bar. As the afternoon progressed, the anecdotes amassed, echoing an email I'd received earlier that week:

"L. said people were really burning out, getting tired, bad things happening, etc. L.—not a paranoid person at all—said he's seen police cars dropping off schizophrenics at the park, and I believed him."

The story varied each time I heard it. That cops were encouraging the chronically-intoxicated and the longtime homeless to head over to Zuccotti. That buses from Rikers were dropping off the recently-bailed two blocks from the park. That protesters in search of police assistance found officers unwilling to help. That the kitchen had cut back on hours to discourage freeloading. Some rumors (the Rikers buses) left me skeptical; others (police encouragement), less so. And while the veracity or falsity of each was impossible to determine with any certainty—they were all hearsay, all third-party accounts—surely there was some truth in what was being said.

I returned home late that evening to see yet another variation reported in the *Daily News* by Harry Siegel: "'He's got a right to express himself, you've got a right to express yourself,'

I heard three cops repeat in recent days, using nearly identical language, when asked to intervene with troublemakers inside the park, including a clearly disturbed man screaming and singing wildly at 3 a.m. for the second straight night."

Let the conflict among them be their own undoing. An old and trusted tactic. Life in the park was undoubtedly becoming more complicated.

On Mon, Oct 31, 2011 at 9:31 PM, Astra Taylor wrote:

Sarah, did you see these? Tweets from a Mother Jones reporter—mention of a possible rape at Zuccotti. I've heard about incidents of sexual harassment, but still I find this hard to believe. But maybe I just don't want to. It's just too awful.

What do you think? And is it responsible for reporters to tweet this kind of speculation, to broadcast gossip?

@JoshHarkinson
A trustworthy #OWS activist tells me that an influx of homeless and hardened criminals is causing major issues for Zuccotti campers

@JoshHarkinson
She cites reports of cops dumping inmates a few blocks away. There are also rumors of NYC's City Homeless Services sending homeless there.

@JoshHarkinson
Most disturbingly, she says there have been reports of rapes at Zuccotti. People are now locking their tents at night.

@JoshHarkinson
If the rogue elements at the park can't be tamed, she thinks #OWS will relocate to a new site that is more easily defended.

On Mon, Oct 31, 2011 at 9:47 PM, Sarah Resnick wrote:

It's hard to imagine with everyone living in such close prox-
imity and the community affairs people up all night, keeping
watch. But anything is possible. I hope it's not true!

And I agree these tweets are irresponsible. That's the dan-
ger of Twitter and the reporters who use it as if they are no
longer reporters. Especially in sensitive situations such as
this one. His followers may retell this information as if it is
fact. And if it doesn't turn out to be true, then . . .

Wednesday, November 2

Astra:

I went down to Wall Street just after 11 AM hoping to catch
the veterans march from the Vietnam memorial, but I was
running a bit late and couldn't find them. No wonder. I later
learned they marched in dignified silence and were, for the
most part, free of a conspicuous police escort. There were no
barricades, no zipcuffs, no orange nets, no authorities with
bullhorns. Only as they approached Zuccotti Park did the
brigade begin to shout, in military cadence: "Corporate profits on the rise, but soldiers have to bleed and die! Sound off,
one, two . . ." Many carried signs that read "I am still serving
my country." Later, when I spot a few servicemen lingering
on Broadway, I am reminded of a federal report on homeless veterans that had been released only days before, which
I read about in the newspaper. There are 144,000 of them, the
experts determined, and they make up a disproportionate
percentage of the homeless population (young veterans are
twice as likely to be homeless as their nonveteran peers) in
part because many have disabilities—both physical and psy-
chological—as a consequence of their military service.

Not just in New York City, but at occupations around the
country, mental health and homelessness have manifested
as interconnected issues, with members of both groups increasingly scapegoated. At Zuccotti Park the homeless are
said to be "occupying the occupation" and are portrayed as

"freeloaders" and "loonies," a danger to the community, a threat to "health and safety" and "quality of life." The homeless are unfairly lumped in with the dangerous, drug-addicted, and, to quote the *New York Post*, "deranged." But housing status and personal conduct aren't the same thing (if nothing else, the elaborate fraud and theft of Wall Street executives should remind us that those who have multiple homes and who appear perfectly sane can be criminal). More importantly, the presence of homeless people at encampments should not be seen as a liability for the movement, but a reminder of why the protest exists, since their condition is directly linked to the unjust and corrupt economic policies OWS is rallying against. Recession-induced homelessness is set to skyrocket over the next five years, and shelters across the country are already filled to capacity with people whose homes have been foreclosed on (in the Midwest, foreclosures are responsible for 15 percent of the newly homeless). Meanwhile, funding for social programs is being chipped away: earlier this year Bloomberg's budget called for a six percent cut in homeless services. In other words, people who should be getting help from the city are instead seeking aid at Zuccotti Park.

Later in the afternoon I introduce two friends so they can talk about bolstering efforts to provide mental health support for people who come to Occupy Wall Street, which has become a veritable tent city, an almost impassable maze of temporary structures housing hundreds on less than an acre. Protesting, especially occupying, entails real strain. It's cold and noisy on the street, which means many occupiers are suffering from sleep deprivation, which compounds other problems. But it's not just the people who are visibly troubled—the ones who are attracting negative press these days—that my one friend is worried about, but regular protesters. "Let's face it," she says, "people with emotional issues end up at this kind of thing." That's not meant to disparage the movement or detract from the cause, she clarifies. It's just to acknowledge that many activists are wounded, broken, and want to fix the world that made them that way. It's

ASTRA TAYLOR & SARAH RESNICK

a kind of sublimation. There's something beautiful about it, but maybe they need help too.

Sarah R:
Oakland general strike today. They've shut down the port. Twitter is going crazy.

@JeffSharlet
Any firm sources on twitter buzz that @occupyoakland protester hit and killed by car, driver released by police? Seems unlikely.

@JeffSharlet
Merc News, MSM, says Mercedes ran red light bcause driver pissed at protesters. Onlookers believe deliberate and acceleration post-impact.

@JeffSharlet
Looking worse. MT @XXX WARNING GRAPHIC! photo of #OccupyOakland protester after hit by car is.gd/x2pNHp

@JeffSharlet
I've been thinking that an Occupy fatality was possible. I thought it would be an overzealous blow w/ a nightstick. Appears it's road rage.

@JeffSharlet
@XXX @XXX @XXX No, I haven't "reported" anything; I'm not there. Trying to sift thru accounts. No death confirmed.

@JeffSharlet
@XXX No deaths. Those rumors were false.

On Thurs, Nov 3, 2011 at 5:45 PM, Astra Taylor wrote:
Reading the news today and talking to people and it appears the stories of sexual assault are true. My fear is that things

will become worthy of a Joan Didion–style essay, a tale of decline and darkness, of dreams turning into nightmares. It's terrible that this happened, but the mayor is making it sound like this sort of shit only goes down at Zuccotti Park (which it doesn't) and, more laughably, that it is only there that it goes unreported when A) these incidents were reported to the police multiple times and B) lots of women don't report attacks out of fear of stigma and shame. I have to admit, I was really hoping this was a fabrication by OWS's enemies, a deception engineered by the rightwing media.

On Thurs, Nov 3, 2011 at 6:33 PM, Sarah Resnick wrote:

This is deeply disturbing, and I worry for the victims. I am also concerned for the broader movement—I hope the press does not blow this up and out of proportion. The individuals responsible for these crimes are by no means representative of OWS, nor are these crimes particular to the park. We're in a large urban center and there is crime throughout this city, every day. In the first three months of 2011 alone, the NYPD reported 340 forcible rapes (which does not include statutory rape and other forms of sexual assault) and it's unlikely that most, if any, of these were covered by the media. I guess what I mean is: I wish we'd spend more time addressing the pervasive cultural tolerance of sexual violence against women rather than spotlight one incident in a park.

And with respect to Bloomberg: As if sexual misconduct is never swept under the rug in the halls of great wealth! We need only look as far back as the coverage of the Dominic Strauss-Kahn case, for instance, which, irrespective of his guilt or innocence, revealed a culture of condonation around sexual predation. Friends like Bernard Henri-Lévy call him "charming, and seductive," while the French essayist Pascal Bruckner pilloried the incident as evidence of our "twisted puritanism" here in the US.

ASTRA TAYLOR & SARAH RESNICK

Friday, November 4

Astra:

Today I heard from folks in Georgia that the little Occupy Athens—which is sometimes only one tent strong—has its share of problems. Last week, when she was visiting, my sister Tara had been distressed because the organizers shooed away a homeless man from the first meeting. Sure, the guy is a notorious alcoholic, she told me, but he's also a sweetheart who has been around for years. She thinks they should have tried to recruit him. Today our houseguests, also from Georgia, tell me about the mini-occupation's tribulations. Supposedly the encampment keeps getting ransacked by homeless men getting up off their benches in the middle of the night and drunkenly rustling through all the coolers and boxes in the food area, making a huge mess while on a hopeful hunt for donuts. Not only that, but the protest also attracts a good number of counter-demonstrators. For example, two straight-looking fellows showed up the other day with "Invade Mexico" signs. My friend claims that Rush Limbaugh has been advising his listeners to infiltrate OWS and stand around with off-message signs to confuse and turn off passersby. "Are you guys here because of Limbaugh?" my houseguest asked the interlopers. They wouldn't respond to the question, she told me, but one of them broke into a wide, mischievous grin. But when I look for evidence that this conspiracy is true—how great it would be if the crazy signs at Zuccotti Park could be blamed on conservative radio cranks!—I can't find any.

Down at Wall Street I run into an ex-coworker, D., now working for the business press. We trade notes on the events of the last six weeks and discuss actions that are being planned. Everyone is gearing up for November 17, the occupation's two-month anniversary. Things need to escalate, we agree, or the media may lose interest; D.'s editors are already saying the protests are old news. D. is excited but also frustrated; so many scoops, but he can't write about them, at least not yet. Right now they are just whispers, designs only beginning to take shape, too premature to make fully public. Things need to stay under the radar a bit longer. Meanwhile, he wants me to call his great uncle and help organize a field trip for a bunch of geriatric radicals since he can't—his job demands the appearance of neutrality. A lot of the residents at his uncle's nursing home are eager to join the protest and they have vans and drivers to bring them to the park. Since it's New York City there must be tons of wizened leftists who would want to join them. Old people want to occupy. Could I help make it happen?

A few feet away a man is speaking, a lawyer, an author, but I don't catch his name. "It's cold down here today," he begins. "It's so cold I saw a bunch of Bank of America lawyers on the corner with their hands in their own pockets."

ASTRA TAYLOR & SARAH RESNICK

On Fri, Nov 4, 2011 at 9:07 PM, Astra Taylor wrote:

Sarah, Are you out and about? I hear that community watch has a meeting at 10pm at the west side of the park and that some important news is being announced.

Friday, November 4

Sarah R:

Friday night at the Tree of Life. The stories around Zuccotti had grown progressively worse that week, though it seemed we'd weathered through it. At the very least, park safety issues were being addressed, and addressed well at that: "safe spaces," including group tents, would be created for people who identified as female; the victims were receiving needed support; and there were trainings around consent and other forms of assault awareness. A security team (a group that prefers to be called "community alliance"), avowedly nonviolent and trained in de-escalation techniques, patrolled the park round the clock, while empowering occupiers to stand up for each other and work with police when need be.

The wind was bitter cold, and we stood with our heads bowed and waited. Occupy Shabbat had just finished a service and we chatted with those who lingered. We'd either missed the meeting or it wasn't happening. I thought of *Much Ado About Nothing*: Had we become Shakespearean characters, steered by rumor and intrigue?

Astra suggested we do a quick tour of the park. At the northeast end, a large group had gathered. Someone was filming and there was a bright light. Before we could hear anything, a large placard: Poetry Assembly. We stood at the edge of the crowd, unsure where to go next, and then decided to stop and listen: "We can fill each other with ourselves . . . Smother my face with your pussy." The words made us cringe; given what may have happened nights before, they seemed particularly ill chosen. But as they were earnestly repeated by the crowd, echoing through the people's microphone, we laughed.

RUMORS

Erin Schell, "Hands and Tents"

BODIES IN PUBLIC

JUDITH BUTLER

Remarks at Zuccotti Park, October 23

I came here to lend my support to you today, to offer my sol-idarity, for this unprecedented display of democracy and popular will. People have asked, "So what are the demands? What are the demands all these people are making?" Either they say there are no demands and that leaves your critics confused—or they say that the demands for social equality and economic justice are impossible demands. And impos-sible demands, they say, are just not practical.

If hope is an impossible demand, then we demand the im-possible. If the right to shelter, food, and employment are impossible demands, then we demand the impossible. If it is impossible to demand that those who profit from the reces-sion redistribute their wealth and cease their greed, then yes, we demand the impossible.

But it is true that there are no demands that you can sub-mit to arbitration here because we are not just demanding economic justice and social equality. We are assembling in public, we are coming together as bodies in alliance, in the street and in the square. We're standing here together making democracy, enacting the phrase "We the people!"

BODIES IN PUBLC

Dan Archer, "Occupied Oakland"

LAUNDRY DAY

KEITH GESSEN

KEITH GESSEN

A young man, maybe thirty years old, clearly from Brooklyn, in a nice fall jacket and hat, gets up to address the General Assembly. "The other day it rained!" he calls out. It's a Sunday in early autumn, a beautiful night, and the GA is packed. The young man has a terrific people's mic delivery. He calls out each sentence dramatically; he has come back from a dark place and needs to tell us his tale.

"The other day it rained!" he says, and everyone repeats it after him.

"A terrible rain!" he emphasizes.

"Many things became wet!

"And dirty!

"They were thrown—into a pile—or discarded.

"And now we have a gigantic mountain!

"Of laundry!

"Maybe you've seen it!

"On the north side of the park!"

An emergency laundry committee has been deputized, he goes on, and it is now asking the General Assembly for funds to truck the mountain of laundry to a laundromat. The young man adds that there will be no exploitation of laundry personnel: the laundry committee will do the laundry themselves; that is, they will put quarters in the machines themselves. They are asking for $3,000.

I look around. By this point I've been to a couple of GAs but have yet to see the question of money come up. And I know OWS is flush with cash—the figure I've heard is around $400,000.

But three thousand dollars? For laundry?

No one comes right out and says so, but it seems like an awful lot of money, and the questions, and the clarifying questions, hint at this concern. Where was the laundry being done? (In Inwood, in northern Manhattan, cheaper than the Financial District.) What would the money be used for? (Mostly quarters, but also a truck to ferry the laundry uptown.) Which truck company was being used, and was it the most economical option? ("I don't know which company is being used. In any case," the young man from the laundry committee adds, a little cryptically, "we have no choice!") Why wasn't this brought up earlier so people could ponder it? (It's an emergency.) At this point the facilitator steps in, perhaps sensing that the crowd is turning against the young man and his proposal, and says he was present at the laundry committee's deliberations. This is the best option, he says, even though it's not ideal.

Someone asks the young man to elaborate about the truck and he does so; the young man has nothing to hide. The truck and its driver have been recommended by a sympathetic labor union and will cost $500. Now we're getting somewhere: the unions are screwing us. Five hundred dollars for a one-day local truck rental? Suddenly a man named Arturo stands up. Arturo has a truck, he declares, and he would be happy to donate it to the occupation for a day. A cheer goes up. Now how much will it cost, the people ask, since the truck and its driver are free?

It will cost the same, says the young man.

How is that possible, he is asked, when Arturo has just knocked $500 off the price?

Arturo's truck is greatly appreciated, says the young man, and it will be useful in the future, but cannot be used in this instance.

Why not?

Because, the young man finally admits, the truck and its driver are already here. The laundry is already being loaded. It was an emergency, and measures have been taken.

The GA takes this in—why have we been arguing about this for an hour if it was already a done deal?—and then goes ahead and votes, though without any particular enthusiasm, to release $3,000 to the emergency laundry committee.

Race

While the great laundry debate is going on, someone circulates a printed sheet describing the proposal for a new spokes council model to replace the General Assembly. They could not have picked a better moment. Clearly the process of taking every single household question before 300 people for discussion is time-consuming and at times counterproductive. But before the new proposal has even been proposed, a beautiful South Asian woman stands up and asks what guarantees there are that the new arrangement would not simply be dominated by white males?

The facilitator, not exactly a white male himself (I learn later that he's Palestinian), takes a long time explaining that this question will need to be addressed in order, through the discussion process, although he recognizes how important it is, in our society, given its history, and so on.

I leave the GA to see if I can get a glimpse of the pile of laundry before it disappears. I make a circle of the park, but it is gone.

When I get back to the GA, it is discussing whether to buy storage bins. A man named Bobby, a former sailor who's on the sanitation crew, stands up in favor of the proposal and delivers a short speech.

"Last week," he says, "we put forward a proposal to buy storage bins. The proposal passed, but with amendments. First, the bins had to be fair trade. Second, they had to be bought on Craigslist.

"This turned out to be impossible."

Bobby sits down.

So I miss the discussion on race. But I have caught some others. Oh, they are tedious, these discussions of race. And if you've been around any kind of activism, you have heard them many, many times before. And yet there's something different this time around, or so it seems to me. People raise the issue; the issue is discussed. Sometimes it gets "dealt" with, sometimes it gets delayed or papered over or whatever. People walk out; people come back. It just somehow doesn't feel as toxic, as destructive, as I remember it feeling the last time I really ran into it, in college in the mid-'90s. And I want to say: Good. They've moved on. *They* aren't going to scuttle everything just so that we can acknowledge some old grievance that

KEITH GESSEN

happened many years before any of us were born, that we can do nothing about, that we are not in a position to apologize for, for which there is no way for us to make amends.

But—that's not what happened, is it? What's happened is that we changed. Or we've begun to. We—white males, I mean—have made the necessary adjustments. Twenty years ago, *they were right and we were wrong*. We were wrong. It might be useful to keep saying that for a while.

Kirill Medvedev

It's easy to forget, if you live in New York, just how terrifying the city can be—especially the Financial District, with its narrow streets, and towers leaning monstrously over them, and the ominous Ground Zero construction, literally across the street from the park, digging into the earth.

"Kostya," the Russian poet Kirill Medvedev says to me when we finally cross Chambers Street and enter the District, "where on earth are we?"

We have walked down from Penn Station, visiting the sites a Russian poet would most enjoy—the Chelsea Hotel, the Stonewall Inn, Joseph Brodsky's old house on Morton Street. Finally we've arrived at the Revolution.

An ordinary Russian poet may scoff, but Kirill is no ordinary Russian poet. He is very active in the nascent (or re-nascent) Russian socialist movement; he and his small Trotskyist group are always holding protests—small, but resonant— against the government and its nasty, anti-human policies, and against art galleries that host neo-fascistic art, and (once) against a theater company that supported the Kremlin but was also staging Brecht.

I leave Kirill alone once we get to Zuccotti so he can walk around. On the way he's been telling me how the Russian government recently fenced off a giant section of Moscow's historic central district for government housing, essentially making that part of the city inaccessible to everyone else. He's been trying to think of a potential Occupy response—though

LAUNDRY DAY

Russian OMON troops can be pretty nasty, and, more to the point, there is a lot of distrust on the side of Moscow's anarchists, who consider the socialists too hierarchical. Among the socialists too there are many arguments about hierarchy.

Kirill likes Zuccotti Park, though I can tell he is put off by its chaos. "They need to come up with demands," he says. "Demands are the key."

That evening I have somewhere to be, and Kirill has to go back to Pennsylvania, to the poetry festival that flew him out here, but before he goes he is able to take in a GA. This is the evening after Oakland is raided by police using tear gas, injuring numerous people, and putting an Iraq War veteran in the hospital with a fractured skull. In solidarity, after the GA, a large contingent of OWSers marches north from Zuccotti to Union Square, shutting down traffic on Broadway and defying the police.

The next day I email Kirill to make sure he caught his train, and also to wonder whether he'd managed to be in the march. He caught his train, he says, and missed the march. "But I did manage to catch the entire discussion"—at the GA—"about whether they should buy some shelves."

Laundry, Part 2

I find myself in Manhattan with a car and 700 copies of the reprinted *Occupy!* gazette in my trunk, so off I go to Zuccotti. It's past midnight and a big friendly guy named Haywood is manning the info booth. Haywood is from North Carolina; he's named after Big Bill Haywood of the Wobblies. He loves *n+1*! He's been living at the park for three weeks now, and he is tired. People show up to help, work awhile, then disappear. The park has become less safe in recent weeks, and Haywood has helped to organize a community watch; it can't do much, but it can keep an eye on the park and call the police if something really bad happens.

Haywood says he enjoys the gazette.

KEITH GESSEN

"There were a lot of typos in the first printing," I say, "but we fixed most of them."

"A lot of typos is better than a lot of lies," says another guy at the info desk, "and that's all we get from Wall Street."

"True," says Haywood, mediating. "But a typo does tear at the heart."

Haywood and his girlfriend Christine and I walk over to the McDonald's on Broadway so she can use the bathroom. This McDonald's is occupied! I have never seen such a thing. It is full of people of every possible description, with ragged coats, crazy hair, a certain number of laptops. Christine uses the restroom; Haywood, meanwhile, competent and gregarious, addresses a security concern with a broad-shouldered colleague holding a walkie-talkie. The colleague points out an older guy whose beard is partly dyed blond: "That guy is either a great actor, or he's nuts," says the security colleague. Haywood takes this under advisement; he then talks with an Asian woman whose purse has been stolen. "We're all burning out," Haywood tells her. She should take a few days off.

Eventually we walk back to the park; Haywood seems as informed about the inner workings of the occupation as anyone I've met, so naturally I ask him what's going on with the laundry. He says the laundry is in some disarray. I say, only half lying, that I have experience handling complex logistical operations. Haywood, diplomatic, says he will keep this in mind.

Working Group

While handing out gazettes in the park I meet a young man named Dale. He's tall, twenty-four, polite, grew up in Indiana and emigrated to Austin a few years ago because he'd heard it was a cool place and there was plenty of work. This turned out to be false. It wasn't that cool—for the most part it was just people getting drunk all the time—and there wasn't that much work: Dale, who hadn't gone to college, ended up working at a call center that raised money for the Democratic Party.

After a while he became a supervisor, so he wasn't cold-calling people all the time, and he'd found it pretty interesting work. "The Democrats are actually more interested in the data than in the money, it seemed to me. You have this huge database of people's responses. Last year, during the healthcare debate, we couldn't raise any money."

"Because people thought Obama was a socialist?"

"No! They thought he wasn't pushing hard enough. There wasn't a public option. People felt betrayed."

Dale has driven up from Austin in a 1978 Mercedes that he outfitted so that it runs on grease. He says when he first made the transition to grease he'd get it directly from restaurants, but after a while he found this too time-consuming, and also the grease wasn't very high quality. Now he buys it on the internet for a dollar a pound. His Mercedes is currently parked in Brooklyn; once a week he takes the subway out and moves it to the other side of the street.

By this point I've figured out that, press and tourists aside, there are three kinds of people in the park at any given time. There are the homeless or lawless who've come for the food and the freedom from police harassment; there are the organizers, both experienced and novice, who are mostly from New York, highly educated, mostly in their late twenties and thirties, and mostly not living in the park. And then there are the kids who actually do live in the park. There's a small overlap of organizers who are also living in the park—Haywood is one; a tall, redheaded guy with a beard named Daniel Zetah is another—but for the most part this split obtains. It's problematic, to a certain extent, but the fact is it's vital that the park continue to be occupied, and the other fact is it's hard to get much done when you're living there. It's hard enough just to avoid hypothermia. I mean, do you live in a park?

But what you think of this split arrangement also depends on what you make of the kids. They're described, even by sympathetic writers, as "anarchists," which I suppose is technically true, but another equally true description would be "twenty-year-olds." What twenty-year-old is not an anarchist? And so

KEITH GESSEN

are these twenty-year-olds, also. But they're much more than that. When you say "anarchist," I hear "nihilist"—like the Black Bloc kids who used to come to the anti-globalization protests just to smash shit. None of the young people I've met at Zuccotti want to smash shit just to smash shit, though they do enjoy smashing shit—or at least taking over the streets—to make a point. They are the opposite of cynical. They actually think that coming to a faraway city and living in a concrete park could lead to political change. And they may be right!

Dale introduced himself to me because of the gazette, not because he wants to write for it but because he is trying to set up an OWS print-shop workers' co-op, and he wonders if we'd consider printing with him. He's read a lot about workers' co-ops, he says, and it seems like there is a great demand for printing work at OWS. Dale asks more questions about printing, and when I run into him a few days later, he asks more questions still—he is about to go off to the Alternative Economies Working Group and wants to give a full report. I offer to come with him and help give the report.

The Alternative Economies Working Group turns out to be quite small—three guys, including Dale, who've been occupying the park, and two other guys from a small NGO called The Working World, which is committed to setting up workers' co-ops around the world. The two guys, college-educated and barely thirty, if that, have spent most of the past decade in Argentina and Nicaragua, but now they are here.

"It's a very different situation," one of them admits.

And it is an interesting meeting. None of the members of the potential print shop has any experience with printing, but they are going to try. There is a space in downtown Brooklyn whose owner is sympathetic to the movement and willing to give them a good price; and one member of the future co-op, Julio, has talked with some OWS organizers to learn where they print, what they are printing, and for how much. The OWS organizer, it turns out, knew what they were printing, but not how much it cost; he just goes to Staples and pays whatever Staples asks. So Julio marched down to Staples. "The guy there got annoyed with all the questions, so he just gave me a bunch of receipts," says Julio, producing a stack of receipts for every imaginable print job—from black-and-white two-sided sheets (seven cents a page) to large full-color glossy posters (a whopping $84 a poster, at least according to the receipts). The OWS organizer also told Julio that they wanted to print stickers, pins, and magnets, but didn't know how—if Julio could figure it out, there'd be some work for the co-op right there.

It's a little puzzling, this meeting. In Argentina and Nicaragua, The Working World presumably deals with workers who have a trade of some kind—carpentry, say—but don't know how to organize themselves, and incorporate, and do marketing—with workers, in short, who have a trade but don't know what a workers' co-op is. Whereas here they are dealing with young people who know all about workers' co-ops but have no trade. When I tell this to my girlfriend, Emily, she says that the solution is for Dale and Julio to go work for Working World. When I tell it to Kirill, he's more sanguine: "It's all right," he says. "We used to not know anything either."

I have to leave the working group early to catch the big community board meeting; it's been rumored that they may pass a resolution condemning the occupation. As I'm getting up, Julio looks at me. "So," he says, quietly, looking down at his receipts and smiling a little into his Che Guevara beard, "how do you think we're doing?"

I tell them what I think, which is that they're doing everything right. They're checking prices, doing research, asking questions. And if Dale can figure out how to make a Mercedes run on grease, he can figure out how to run a printing press.

Community

But of course it's not easy to set up a small business when you're living in a park.

The community board meeting is at a high school at the northern edge of the Financial District, and I'm a little late walking into the school auditorium, a school auditorium like any other (and what did I think, that it'd be made of gold?). "I find this resolution shocking," a man is saying. "This is a perversion of the First Amendment. The First Amendment does not protect making noise and urinating and defecating all over our neighborhood. I say, not in our backyard!"

Some people cheer. I take a seat and figure that one after another, concerned neighbors will get up and say something similar. And a number of them do. So do small business owners: A restaurant owner says that occupiers have been coming in with pots and pans and filling them up with water in his bathroom (and he pays good money for that water); he also says his employees don't feel safe walking home at night. But it turns out that anyone is allowed to get up and speak, including people with only a tangential relationship to the neighborhood. A woman who lives nearby and often bikes through the neighborhood gives a moving speech about taking her daughter by the protests and explaining to her that "sometimes, in America, people do things that are illegal because they believe them to be necessary. Rosa Parks, for example, who refused to give up her seat on a bus." The woman, who is in her forties, says she too was once part of an illegal encampment: at Yale, in the early '80s, to pressure the university to divest from South Africa.

There has been a great deal of fear at OWS about this meeting—negotiations with the drummers, to get them to ease up, had apparently broken down, with at least one of the Dans from the info desk telling me that he'd gone over there one evening to ask them to quiet down and been physically attacked. An email has circulated saying that the drummers are about to destroy the entire movement—that the neighbors are going to withdraw their support. And of course who cares about the bourgeois neighbors, but, as any guerrilla movement can tell you, the sympathy of the local population is crucial.

At the community board meeting, it's not clear at all that the various effects of drum mediation have any relevance. There are other forces at work. In addition to the neighborhood residents (mostly there to voice their complaints), the

LAUNDRY DAY

non-residents (there to voice their support), and the actual occupiers (there mostly to introduce themselves—"I sympathize about the noise," says one, "it's even louder where I am, believe me"; "I got a library card," says another, "I'm part of your community now"), there are the representatives of various New York politicians. Each and every one of them is here to praise the community board for its wise resolution, which does ask the protesters to keep the drumming to a minimum, and to stop pissing and shitting on the streets and in the stairwells of the neighborhood, but also asks police to remove barricades throughout the neighborhood and generally to chill out. What is clearest in that school auditorium is that no Democratic politician wants to be on the wrong side of Occupy Wall Street. They are afraid of the consequences. Will they stay afraid? I don't know. And I don't know if the meeting of a community board in a neighborhood where the average apartment probably costs a million dollars is what democracy looks like. But it does give some clues to what political power looks like, and what it requires (people on the streets), and what it can, at least temporarily, do.

The resolution, to continue to welcome the protesters, overwhelmingly passes.

KEITH GESSEN

NPR

I turn on NPR for the first time in weeks; it's their weekly news quiz show, "Wait Wait . . . Don't Tell Me!" Lately, like in the past year, I've been finding the show, along with just about every other NPR show, irritating to the point of distraction—I wish they would stop trying to charm me for just a second and tell me the goddamn news. But the introduction promises that they're going to talk about OWS, and I keep it on as I drive into the city. The segment on OWS is partly about the drumming controversy (they quote a drummer saying of the organizers, "They've turned into the government that we've been trying to protest!") and also in general about how the protesters have become stinky from eating lentil soup and not showering. They make fun of the protests, but in a good-natured way, and I find myself imagining what it's like to only hear about them on NPR and read about them in the *Times*. So it's a group of smelly hippies occupying a park, worrying about their drum circle, making somewhat incoherent political statements. It's not a bunch of Bertrand Russells sleeping in those tents. And yet they're demanding the things that one oneself wants, that one could never quite admit to wanting before. They are speaking the words that lie frozen inside the hearts of people who listen to NPR. I feel like, for now, that's how it looks from the outside—and that's not bad.

Ray

We have the first strategy session for the "writers and artists affinity group" on Saturday, October 29, the coldest and ugliest day of the year. In the morning it is cold and rainy; by early afternoon it has begun to snow, in thick, wet, ugly snowflakes. We meet in the atrium of 60 Wall Street, like a real live working group, and discuss various direct actions we might take, as writers, to bring attention to the things we find troubling—the decline of bookstores, the defunding of public libraries. In the end the meeting is hijacked by anarchists (well, just one anarchist, it is a small meeting), who wants to hold a shield-making party, and an older Asian-American artist and organizer, who joins the meeting to tell us about some Third World artists he is bringing over to make art about the occupation. He says he doesn't usually work with white people but he is willing to on this project, since it is so important. Though, he adds, it's not like he has anything against white people. "Some of my friends are Jews," he says.

"We're not *all* Jewish," says David Marcus, one of the writers.

"Well, whatever," says the artist, and of course he is right. We decide to hold a shield-making party at the end of the week.

Afterward I head into the park to hand out some gazettes. It is too wet and cold to do so; the park looks deserted, though presumably there are people hiding out in their tents. Daniel at the info desk tells me to come back tomorrow when it's nicer.

I duck into a Starbucks to get a coffee and warm up before going home. The place is filled with Chinese tourists and a few occupiers; the occupiers have laptops, the tourists have cameras and iPads. One older man, in his fifties, with a short gray beard and gray hair, is standing near an electrical outlet, where his smartphone is charging up. He is not dressed for the cold and his jeans are frayed at the cuffs. When one of the Chinese tourists starts looking around the Starbucks for a bathroom, he tells her there isn't one. "There's one in the other Starbucks, around the corner," he says. "But the best one is in Century 21, just up Broadway. There's never a line. I've been living in the park for three weeks," he says, laughing, "and I know all the best spots."

The Chinese tourist—she turns out to be a Chinese journalist, actually—goes off to find the bathroom, and I invite the man to sit down. He is Ray, from Seattle. He lived there all his life, working mostly as a techie—general computer stuff, a lot of design work. But recently work had been drying up, and as time passed things weren't getting any better. Some months ago he began selling off his belongings to pay his rent. He sold his iPad; he sold his sound system. Eventually he sold everything and with the last of his money bought a $250 bus ticket to New York. It wasn't easy to sleep on the bus, Ray tells me, but it wasn't nearly as lousy a journey as he'd been led to expect.

He is articulate, thoughtful, the former owner—this thought actually goes through my mind—of an iPad. It is a little hard to wrap one's head around, but Ray now has nowhere to live. He has no job, no way of making money, and Zuccotti Park, for all its charms, isn't exactly the ideal venue from which to begin looking for a way to turn things around. Or maybe it is, who knows. At least as long as the occupation lasts, Ray has a place to stay.

We exchange phone numbers and emails (Ray even tells me his Twitter handle), and I ask what he plans to do tonight: it's miserable out. He says he'll probably do what he did last time it was cold and rainy, which is ride the subway all night. "But you can't sleep on the subway," I say. "Yes," says Ray, "I stay awake."

When I get home I ask Emily if we can invite Ray to stay the night. She says of course. I email him, and forty-five minutes later he is ringing our doorbell, and a minute after that we've hustled him into the shower. "How was it?" I ask when he gets out (in truth the drain hasn't been draining as well as it should).

"Amazing!" says Ray, heading for his smartphone. "I haven't showered in three weeks. I need to tweet it."

Over tea, Ray tells me a little more about his life. He is from a small family; after his parents died a few years ago, he and his sister drifted apart. His parents were themselves from a small town in the Midwest, they had come to the big city and started a small business. So Ray never knew his extended family, and what's more both he and his sister had been adopted. In recent years, he says, as work had dried up, he'd become something of a hermit, mostly reaching out to the world through social media and his blog.

The next day, I read through Ray's blog. It's a pretty typical blog, at first. Ray has some TV shows he likes, *Breaking Bad* in particular, and he says clever things about them. He's also increasingly angry about the political direction of the country; his favorite pundit is Rachel Maddow.

There aren't very many entries, and the focus of a lot of them is Ray's frustration that he's not keeping up with his blog entries. This sounds a little funny, maybe, because who cares, but not being able to do something you want to do, whether or not it's objectively important, suggests that there's something else going wrong. Then there is a long gap between entries; then an entry indicating, for the first time, that Ray may be in financial trouble; and then:

About to board a bus to NYC. Not sure if I'll ever come back to Seattle.

As a notoriously unsentimental person I can't feel bad about leaving. I've loved living here, was born here. Lived within a few miles from where I was born almost all of my life. That kinda makes me sad. I had opportunities to explore but chose to remain comfortably here.

Now I must leave.

New York is someplace I've always wanted to see. I'm sure I'm thoroughly unprepared for it which makes me want to go there all the more.

I was asked why I would choose to be homeless somewhere like New York rather than stay here. I honestly would find being homeless in Seattle far too depressing. At least by going to New York I'm going somewhere I've always wanted to see.

I have had some moments of panic, asking myself if I've completely lost my mind. That's entirely possible. But those moments pass quickly and my sense of adventure takes over and I'm ready to hit the road all the more.

This may sound strange but the people I'm really going to miss are the baristas at the Tully's on 47th, the checkout clerks at the Safeway on 15th, and the counter people at Dick's Drive-In on Queen Anne. There are lots of others but I frequented those places more than any others and was always treated as a welcome regular and friend.

I'm going to try to update my status as often as possible though it's impossible to say when or where I'll have free wi-fi and my cell is not a very capable conduit to the outside world.

Time to get on the bus soon.

See ya Seattle!

And then there's nothing for three and a half weeks (Ray's laptop was stolen, or simply lost, pretty much as soon as he showed up in the park—"it may still be there," he says, "sometimes people just move stuff and then you don't know where it is"), until Ray checks in.

My situation? I'm homeless, jobless, pretty much penniless and have lost pretty much everything I brought with me. Even with all that life occupying wall street couldn't be more of an adventure. An adventure I'm (but for the occasionally icky weather) enjoying a great deal.

We eat breakfast, do a quick load of Ray's laundry, and then he heads back to the park.

A few days later, I go there with the hope of helping out with the laundry, only to become embroiled in a multi-hour episode involving a methadone addict who is attacked in the park and spirited, for his own safety, to South Ferry Terminal, where Michael, a young stage actor from Chicago, and I have to go looking for him, because the person escorting him is our laundry partner. As all this is going on Michael tells me he's become increasingly frustrated with the occupation, which he's been watching grow more violent and unsafe, and which is spending so much time simply maintaining itself ("bare life," one friend later complains) that it can't even think of effecting political change. "The Super Committee is meeting right now!" he says—meaning, it takes me a second to realize, the Congressional committee on cutting the debt—and meanwhile he's driving a giant truck filled with dirty laundry to northern Manhattan. Because, I discover, that's the way they're doing laundry now: renting a U-Haul, driving it up to Inwood, then spending as many hours as it takes to wash it all. As Michael tells me this, Russell Simmons shows up in the park. "Let's see if I can get a high five," Michael says, moving in his direction. He does not manage a high five. Michael returns and says he's hoping to organize a ten-day march to Washington, DC, to arrive at Congress at the conclusion of the Super Committee deliberations. "Good luck!" I think. About a week later, I will watch TV footage online of Michael carrying an American flag as he leads a group of other protesters onto a ferry bound for New Jersey, to start their long march.

In the meantime, back in Zuccotti, there is a new mountain of dirty laundry. I run into Haywood after the South Ferry

LAUNDRY DAY

debacle and tell him the story. "Typical," he says. But, I add, the Inwood method is not as crazy as I had initially thought. "Also typical," says Haywood.

There must be a better way of doing the laundry, I think. We have not found it yet. But we will.

Illustration by Molly Crabapple

THE AMERICAN CRISIS

THOMAS PAINE

From a winter address, written 235 years ago; read aloud, by order of George Washington, to the encampment at Valley Forge.

December 19, 1776

The summer soldier and the sunshine patriot will, in this crisis, shrink from the service of his country; but he that stands it NOW, deserves the love and thanks of man and woman. Tyranny, like hell, is not easily conquered; yet we have this consultion with us, that the harder the conflict, the more glorious the triumph. What we obtain too cheap, we esteem too lightly. . . . Whether the Independence of the Continent was declared too soon, or delayed too long, I will not now enter into as an argument. . . . We did not make a proper use of last winter, neither could we, while were in a dependent state. However, the fault, if it were one, was all our own; we have none to blame but ourselves. . . .

I once felt all that kind of anger, which a man ought to feel, against the mean principles that are held by the Tories: A noted one, who kept a tavern at Amboy, was standing at his door, with as pretty a child in his hand, about eight or nine years old, as most I ever saw, and after speaking his mind as freely as he thought was prudent, finished with this unfatherly expression, "Well! give me peace in my day." [A] generous parent would have said, "If there must be trouble, let it be in my day, that my child may have peace."

THOMAS PAINE

CONTRIBUTORS

Carla Blumenkranz *is the managing editor of* n+1.

Judith Butler *is Maxine Elliot Professor in the Departments of Rhetoric and Comparative Literature at UC Berkeley.*

Angela Davis *is a teacher, writer, scholar, and activist/ organizer.*

Jodi Dean *teaches political and media theory in Geneva, New York.*

Celeste Dupuy-Spencer *is an artist who lives and works in New York City.*

Keith Gessen *is a founding editor of* n+1.

Zoltán Glück *is pursuing a doctorate in anthropology at the CUNY Graduate Center.*

Mark Greif *is a founding editor of* n+1.

Elizabeth Gumport *is an associate editor of* n+1.

Doug Henwood *is editor of the* Left Business Observer.

Christopher Herring *is pursuing a doctorate in sociology at UC Berkeley.*

L.A. Kauffman *is an activist and organizer.*

Svetlana Kitto *is a writer, teacher, and oral historian living in New York City.*

Sarah Leonard *is an editor at* Dissent *magazine and* The New Inquiry.

Kung Li *is the former executive director of the Southern Center for Human Rights in Atlanta.*

Audrea Lim *is an associate editor at Verso Books.*

Manissa Maharawal *is a graduate student at the CUNY Graduate Center, a writer and an activist.*

Thomas Paine *was a writer and revolutionary.*

Sarah Resnick *is a senior editor at* Triple Canopy.

Marco Roth *is a founding editor of* n+1.

Nikil Saval *is an associate editor of* n+1.

Eli Schmitt *is a writer living in New York.*

Marina Sitrin *is a writer, activist, lawyer, and dreamer, as well as a postdoctoral fellow at the CUNY Graduate Center.*

Astra Taylor *is the director of the documentary films* Zizek! *and* Examined Life.

Sunaura Taylor *is an artist, writer, and activist living in Oakland, CA.*

Rebecca Solnit *is the author of 13 books, including* A Paradise Built in Hell *and* Hope in the Dark.

Stephen Squibb *is pursuing a doctorate in English at Harvard University.*

Alex Vitale *is an associate professor of sociology at Brooklyn College.*

Slavoj Žižek *is a Slovenian philosopher and cultural critic. His books include* Living in the End Times, *and* First as Tragedy, Then as Farce.

With thanks to Jacob Stevens, Andy Hsiao, Zoe Ward, Kathleen Ross, Bryce Bennett, Kaitlin Phillips, David Wescott, Namara Smith, Chris Glazek, Nick Serpe and the other *Dissent* editors, Kelli Anderson, Josh MacPhee, Dan O. Williams.

Royalties from the sale of this book will go to Occupy Wall Street